RETIRE INSP!RE 2

22 Experts Share Their Best Advice
On How Professionals Can Achieve
A Totally Fulfilling Retirement

WM

Retire Inspire 2

First published in June 2025

W&M Publishing

ISBN 978-1-917265-50-8

A CIP catalogue record for this book is available from the British Library.

Contents

5 Welcome To Retire Inspire 2

9 **BD Dalton**
The Longevity Advantage

19 **Sue Belton**
Your One Wild And Precious Life

27 **Vicki Wusche**
Retire With Purpose: The Clarity Code
For A Life You Choose

41 **Chris Beesley And Susan Beesley**
Hybrid Retirement – The Best Of Both Worlds

53 **Anne Taylor**
If Not Now, When? Finances, Fun, And Freedom
In Retirement And Life

63 **Carol A Vincie**
I Failed Retirement And This Is What I Discovered

71 **Andrew Middleton**
Retirement Wasn't For Me,
So I Created Something Better

79 **Sandi Goddard**
A Smallholding In Dorset... Maybe Not!

89 **Ashley Edwards**
From Fear To Freedom

99 **Carl Adamson**
Retirement Is Not A Bed of Roses
For A Serial Entrepreneur

109 **Kath Reade**
Let Your Heart Sing

117 **Jessica McGregor Johnson**
Retirement A Loss Or A Gain? Your Choice

127 **Karen Frith**
Between Two Generations

137 **Steven Shove**
Nesting For Old Age Wasn't For Me -
Three Ideas For Early Retirement

147 **Catherine Rolt**
Retiring Well... The Transition To The Next Chapter

157 **Louise Baker**
Not Retired, Not Late, Not Lazy –
Just Wired Differently, Even Now

165 **Menno Siebenga**
When It Feels Like The Beginning Of The End...
Some Forget To Live – Others Choose To Forget
To Grow Old. The Choice Is Yours.

175 **Lathi Dube**
Rollercoaster Or Walk In The Park: Your Choice

183 **Amanda Hart**
Rewire Before You Retire

191 **Jeff Buehner**
How to Retire

203 **Andrew Priestley**
The Real Retirement Challenge

Welcome To Retire Inspire 2

Retirement. For some, it's a long-anticipated reward for decades of hard work. For others, it's an unnerving leap into the unknown. Whether you've spent your life climbing the corporate ladder or building a business from the ground up, one truth remains: what comes next matters.

Retire Inspire 1 launched in 2019 at the start of Covid.

It *immediately* resonated with those facing redundancy or early retirement. Following the success of the original *Retire Inspire 1* – an international bestseller that struck a chord with professionals around the world – this much-anticipated, updated follow-up volume goes even deeper.

You'll find new stories, fresh voices, and candid insights that reflect the evolving landscape of retirement in our time.

Once again, *Retire Inspire 2* is a timely, thoughtful, and practical companion for anyone within ten years of retirement age – whether you're employed, self-employed, or somewhere in between.

Once again, 21 contributors, share their current best thinking shaped by hard-earned experience and generous reflection. What I absolutley love about this new volume is the incredible broad and varied range of life experience and wisdom, and right across the spectrum of contemplating retirement, in the process of retiring and retired very well! There is literally something here for everyone. You are spoiled for choice

Some of these contributors have spent 30 or 40 years in employment, steering successful careers in complex organisations. Others have created and led businesses of their own – experiencing the highs, the risks, and the quiet resilience it takes to be your own boss. All of them now find themselves navigating the same big questions:

What now? What next? How do I do this well?

This is not a book of theory or platitudes. It's a collection of lived experience, practical strategies, and honest reflections from people who have walked the talk. Whether they're building second-act businesses, healing after burnout, or guiding others through financial transitions, each contributor speaks with the quiet authority of someone who has asked hard questions and made intentional choices.

The stories within this book are diverse and real. You'll find practical advice on investment and pensions. Insights into physical and mental well-being. Reflections on the emotional process of leaving behind an identity built around work. And plenty of inspiration on finding purpose, passion, and even profitable side hustles after the "main event" has ended.

This is not a book about slowing down.

It's about shifting gears. Rethinking what success looks like. Designing a life that reflects your values, your energy, and your dreams—whether that means part-time work, volunteering, travel, mentorship, or something entirely new.

If you are five or ten years away from the traditional retirement age of 65, *Retire Inspire 2* is your timely invitation to pause and reflect. Not to down-tools. But to look ahead with curiosity and certainty.

These stories will challenge you to consider:

What kind of life do I want next?

What do I need to put in place today to make that a reality?

I encourage you to read it slowly, reflect deeply, and – most importantly – take action. Let these stories help you make decisions now that your future self will thank you for.

Retirement isn't the end of your story. It's the start of a new chapter. And again, *Retire Inspire 2* offers the insight and encouragement to write it well.

Let each voice encourage you to think deeply about the life you're designing—financially, emotionally, and creatively.

This book is especially about smarter, conscious choices. Every authoir in this volume is urging you to pause and play.

Importantly, let them inspire you to act now, not later.

Andrew Priestley

Editor

The Longevity Advantage: What If The Playbook For Retirement Looked Different?

BD Dalton II

Meet Billy O'School. Billy followed the retirement playbook religiously: forty years at the same firm, gold watch at 65, pension pot carefully preserved. He was the poster child for industrial age thinking, loyal, steady, predictable.

At 72, he's mastered the art of the early bird special and can recite every *Coronation Street* plotline from the past decade. His biggest thrill? Debating whether his savings will outlast his hip replacement. His biggest fear? Running out of either money or purpose before his body gives out.

Living the dream, right? More like a nightmare.

Now meet Jan and Dave Long. Same age, completely different game. Just back from consulting wine producers in Southern France. Next week? The are part of a launch of a sustainable food startup with their 28-year-old business partner. Their retirement plan? They've got four, and counting. They never planned to escape work; they designed work to evolve with them. Busy people get things done.

The difference isn't luck or privilege. It's strategy, perseverance and optimism.

While Billy optimized for safety and predictability, Jan and Dave optimized for adaptability and growth. They understood something most people miss: longer lives require bigger thinking, not just bigger pension pots. The best part about this is that you can get around some of the challenges of agism by becoming your own boss.

These are case studies in the biggest wealth opportunity most people are ignoring: planning for a 100-year life.

The New Math Of Living

By 2050, hitting 100 will be routine, not remarkable. Life expectancy doubled between 1900 and 2000, and the curve keeps climbing. When will it stop? Stanford University calls it "designing long life," but for entrepreneurs like us it's the ultimate strategic advantage, if you're willing to ditch the one-and-done retirement model. If you don't make 100 that is okay, but if you do and you don't plan for it, yikes.

Think about the math. If you're 45 today, you probably have 50-ish productive years ahead of you. That's more than most people's entire working lifetime a century ago. The question isn't whether you can afford to retire, it's whether you can afford to waste five decades sitting on the sidelines.

Jan and Dave cracked this code early. Their first "retirement" happened at 47 when they sold their marketing agency. But instead of buying a boat and sailing into the sunset, they invested time in themselves. Dave dove into Italian cooking in Tuscany while Jan studied sustainable agriculture in Costa Rica. The result? Not just Instagram memories, but a wildly successful organic restaurant chain that generated more wealth than their original agency. They both did these with different people, which expanded the circle of acquaintances and influence.

That business funded their next pivot at age 65: teaching, writing, mentoring. Their Southeast Asia travels weren't tourism, they were R&D that led to new intellectual property and consulting revenue. Each move built on the last, creating compound returns that went far beyond financial. Each interaction expanded their circle of influence and challenged their brains, which led to prolonging their mental capacity and reducing the onset of cognitive disorders, as a side effect, rather than being the reason they did it.

Here's what most people miss: they treated each transition as a strategic business decision, not an emotional reaction to burnout or boredom. They planned their sabbaticals like other people plan IPOs.

Each strategic pause wasn't winding down, it was repositioning for relaunch. That cookbook and teaching tour? Over £200,000 in fees. Now in their seventies, they're working smarter than ever: part-time, on their terms, solving problems they care about, building something that outlives them.

Meanwhile, Billy's watching the clock run down on a finite pot of money, increasingly disconnected from a world that moved on without him. The gap between these approaches compounds every year. Billy's story gets smaller; Jan and Dave's keeps becoming the thing their friends look at and aspire to follow.

The Compound Effect Of Reinvention

The real difference is financial architecture and what we call a *longevity plan*, which looks at Life Span, Wealth Span, and Health Span. Billy saved into a shrinking pot. Every year, less money. Jan and Dave built cascading income streams where each phase funded the next. Agency exit paid for a sabbatical and seeded the restaurant. Restaurant funded the publishing phase. Publishing phase funded the current startup.

Value multiplied, not just preserved.

This isn't just about having more money; it's about having more options. When your income comes from multiple sources across different time horizons, you're not just wealthy, you're antifragile. Market crashes? You've got other streams. Industry disruption? You're already diversified. Health issues? Systems run without you so the focus is on health.

Even their networks compound differently. Billy's inner circle is mostly other retirees debating healthcare costs and complaining about "kids these days." Jan and Dave built what Stanford researchers call a "multi-generational brain trust". Their team includes a 28-year-old tech specialist, 45-year-old CFO, 68-year-old mentor who's survived five economic cycles, and an 82-year-old wine distributor with contacts from Napa to Bordeaux.

Age-diverse teams consistently outperform monoculture ones in both creativity and results. When you're solving for a 50-year business horizon, you need perspectives that span decades. The 28-year-old sees opportunities the 68-year-old might miss. The 68-year-old spots risks the 28-year-old hasn't lived through yet. Together, they're unstoppable.

Travel As A Business Strategy

Billy treated holidays like *escapes* - same beach, same fortnight, same paperbacks. Now retirement feels like one endless, dull staycation. When every day is Saturday no day feels special.

Jan and Dave? Every trip was market research. Thirties for exploring opportunities. Forties for studying global trends. Fifties for building supplier relationships. Sixties and seventies for turning adventures into revenue streams through consulting, speaking, writing. Every journey either sparked ideas or strengthened partnerships. Many paid for themselves. Others launched entirely new chapters.

The difference is *intentionality.* Billy consumed experiences. Jan and Dave invested in them. One approach costs money; the other makes it.

The Multi-Arc Career Strategy

Stop seeing retirement as the finish line. A 100-year life means multiple career peaks.

In your twenties and thirties, focus on learning and experimentation. Your forties and fifties become prime time to scale, lead, and cash in. Your sixties and seventies? That's when wisdom pays dividends, patterns emerge, and legacy partnerships take root. Your eighties and beyond? That's when you become the elder statesman everyone wants to learn from.

But none of this happens if you cling to the myth that age equals irrelevance. In knowledge, work especially, experience compounds. The best consultants, advisers, and dealmakers often hit their stride well past traditional retirement age.

They've seen every cycle, navigated every crisis, and built relationships that span decades.

Jan and Dave used each decade strategically. J&D Marketing Agency thrived on hustle and grit. Their restaurant scaled through systems and relationships. The food startup draws on deep experience, lifetime learnings, and networks money can't buy. Billy played it safe, but safe in a long-life economy often means stale, and eventually, stranded.

Here's the counterintuitive truth: **the riskiest strategy in a 100-year life is playing it safe.**

Inflation alone will eat your purchasing power. Technology will make your skills obsolete. Markets will shift beneath your feet. The only real security comes from staying relevant, connected, and valuable.

Rethinking Financial Planning

Traditional retirement planning assumes a fixed pot stretching 30+ years. What if instead you created five distinct income arcs? Not every reinvention needs to be a unicorn. Sometimes it's consulting. Sometimes it's partnering with someone younger but less connected. Sometimes it's licensing your expertise or monetizing your network. The trick isn't just staying in the game; it's changing the game as your assets evolve.

Consider this: Warren Buffett made 90% of his wealth after age 65. Mandatory retirement would have cost him billions and deprived the world of decades of wisdom. Laura Ingalls Wilder didn't publish her first *Little House* book until she was 64. Frank Lloyd Wright designed Guggenheim Museum at 76.

These aren't exceptions, they're previews of what's possible when you design for longevity instead of limiting yourself by outdated age assumptions.

Community becomes capital. Billy retired into isolation. Jan and Dave expanded into ecosystems spanning generations, industries, and continents. Their 20-year-old collaborators become 40-year-old partners.Their 60-year-old mentors become 80-year-old allies. That continuity isn't just nice, it's profitable.

In a 100-year business plan, relationships are your most valuable asset. They appreciate over time, compound in value, and can't be replicated by competitors. The executive you mentor today might offer you a board seat tomorrow. The startup founder you advise in their twenties might acquire your company in their forties. The peer you collaborate with across decades becomes your business partner for life.

Your Strategic Audit

Step One: Examine Your Trajectory

This is not your business plan. Are you building one long grind toward a golf course, or a series of arcs with fresh energy and upside? Are you cultivating networks that challenge your thinking, or just echo chambers of the things you believe in too? Are you designing roles that strengthen with age, or ones that force you out when you've finally got your best moves?

Step Two: Map Your "Next Retirements."

Don't wait for 65 to reinvent. AI is accelerating this.

Look ahead ten years. What new chapter could build on today's assets? Could you invest in a protégé, explore new markets, or take strategic breaks to gather insights? The new life map includes multiple transitions. Start planning them now.

Make sure you learn about AI. You don't have to know everything, but an understanding will go a really long way.

The Choice

Simple fork in the road: Billy's slow fade... or the Longs' next adventure? One path leads to safety but also stagnation.

The other *seems* riskier, yes, but the rewards run deeper.

You'll likely live longer than your parents, probably longer than you're planning for. The real question isn't whether you'll last longer, it's whether you'll matter longer.

The longevity advantage isn't about living longer. It's about earning longer. Design your bonus decades and they will be your most engaging and lucrative chapter yet.

What's your next act going to be?

About B.D.

Barton 'B.D.' Dalton II AKA 'The Lazy Over-Achiever' brings over 25 years of expertise across financial and business sectors. He has built successful enterprises spanning the United States and Europe, including Temple Row Wealth Management and Rockfine Group, while serving as CEO of a legal practice.

B.D. leverages his extensive business knowledge through nationwide speaking engagements, workshops, conferences, and coaching sessions. His business acumen is captured in three published books: *The Assisted Purchase, True Gravity,* and his bestseller *Grow, Sell and Retire*, which share logical, tried-and-tested strategies and systems.

The success of *Grow, Sell and Retire* led to a thriving podcast series of over 150 episodes, where B.D. hosts conversations with industry-leading guests, sharing practical business insights and proven methodologies.

Website: *https://www.rockfine.co.uk*

X: *https://x.com/GrowSellRetire*

YouTube: *https://www.youtube.com/channel/UCBhSWdxovOODxClKv3m29tQ*

LinkedIn: *https://www.linkedin.com/company/rockfine-group/*

Your One Wild And Precious Life

Sue Belton

There's a question I've started asking more often. Not just of clients, but of myself too:

"What do you want to look back on and be glad you did?"

It cuts through the noise. Through status. Through years of striving. It gets to the heart of what this next chapter - retirement or something like it - is really about.

I've spent my career surrounded by high-achieving men in their 40s and 50s: finance execs, engineers, construction leaders. Brilliant, driven, respected. And utterly depleted.

They come to me when something cracks. When they've been in overdrive for years and can no longer remember why. They say things like, "I'm just holding on until I can retire." But what they really mean is, "I've lost touch with what matters."

The world celebrates their work ethic. But it rarely sees the price: missed birthdays, health scares, numb marriages, joyless Sundays. I see it all. I've lived parts of it too.

I sacrificed a lot in the first act of my life. Health. Fun. Time with the people I love. I wore busy like a badge of honour. I believed, like many do, that success meant always doing more.

And I was good at it. I built a strong reputation. But I also lost things I'll never get back.

Now, early fifties, I'm choosing differently. I've created a detailed three-year vision and a broader plan for the next decade. This isn't about retiring. It's about reshaping. Reclaiming. Rebalancing.

I'm not stepping back. I'm stepping *into* something fuller, freer, and more honest.

To anchor this shift, I use a framework I call the **Six Fs**. These aren't just ideas - they're how I live now, and how I guide others through this transition.

1. Fitness

We only get one body. The condition of that body will define the quality of our retirement. I've trained regularly since my twenties - though I was that asthmatic 1970s kid who was told to avoid sport. Now, I work with Jack Coxall of Fitness Lab, who reminds me that joint replacements and loss of mobility aren't inevitable. With weight-bearing work and functional movement, we can build strength and preserve freedom. Retirement shouldn't shrink our lives. It should expand them.

Fitness isn't just about the gym. It's stamina for life - hiking, carrying grandchildren, dancing at weddings. It's about feeling good in your own skin. About trusting your body. That's a form of self-respect I didn't fully understand until recently. And I want others to know it's never too late to start.

2. Faith

Not religion - though it might be for some. For me, faith is about purpose, meaning, contribution. It's about believing there's more to life than ticking boxes.

When I became a coach 17 years ago, I found my purpose: to show people they always have a choice. That they can rewrite their story. That's the kind of legacy I want to leave. Not just in my work, but in the business I'm building to outlast me - one I'll remain involved in as a mentor and advisor.

It's also about trust. Trust in the unknown. Trust that stepping away from an old version of success won't mean failure. It might mean something deeper. More grounded. More real.

3. Finance

For most of my life, I was financially independent. I've worked hard, stood on my own feet, and made my way. Now, planning a future with my soon-to-be husband, I've entered a new chapter: shared finances, joint goals. We worked through Ramit Sethi's *Money For Couples* and built a financial vision that reflects what matters to us.

For me, money's always been about freedom. In this next phase, that freedom needs to support a life of purpose, connection, generosity and fun - not just survival.

Retirement planning isn't just about having enough. It's about designing a life you're excited to fund. A life that includes adventure. Kindness. Rest. Space.

4. Family

This one's everything. I have a daughter who's nearly 20. I'm gaining stepchildren and grandchildren. I want to be present. I want to give time, not just what's left over. I know that for many, this time of life includes loss - divorce, distance, shifts in family structure. I'm fortunate to be in a relationship that's deepening.

I'm choosing to nurture it every day. Family isn't just what we're given. It's what we build.

It's not just about being there. It's about being really there. Phone down. Eyes up. Willing to play, talk, rest. That's where meaning lives.

5. Friends

As an only child, my friends have always been my chosen family. These women are my sisters. My constants. The ones who've known every version of me and loved me through all of them. As I get older, I want more time with them. Not squeezed in. Prioritised.

There's something sacred about friendships now. We've lived through things. We know what matters. These connections don't just support us - they shape us. They are the foundation.

6. Fun!

This has been my biggest shift. I was a workaholic. Fun wasn't just missing - I had no idea how to do it. It felt wasteful. Then my late friend Judy gave me a gift. In her final days, she left behind a simple message: "Organised fun."

Not fun as an afterthought. Fun as a practice. Something you schedule. Protect. Prioritise.

That message cracked something open. Now, fun is essential. It's how I know I'm alive. I say yes more. I laugh louder. I let go sooner. Because life isn't just about getting through. It's about enjoying it while we're here.

I share all of this not as a formula, but as an invitation.

One of my clients, a senior executive, once told me he was working 70-hour weeks just to make it to 55 and retire. He was drained. Disconnected. Missing his children's lives. I asked him, "What do you want to be glad about on your deathbed?"

He paused. Then said:

"I want to be glad I changed. That I saw what mattered before it was too late. That I didn't miss it."

That's where it starts. Not with numbers. But with honesty.

Your Turn

Use the Six Fs to reflect and get honest with yourself:

- **Fitness:** What will your body need from you to stay strong and free?
- **Faith:** What gives your life meaning?
- **Finance:** Is your money supporting the life you want?
- **Family:** Who do you want to be more present for?
- **Friends:** Who lifts you up? Are you prioritising them?
- **Fun:** When did you last laugh, play, feel joy?

And the most important question:

What do you want to look back on and be glad you did?

According to *The Top Five Regrets of the Dying* by Bronnie Ware who interviewed people in palliative care:

1. I wish I'd had the courage to live a life true to myself.
2. I wish I hadn't worked so hard.
3. I wish I'd had the courage to express my feelings.
4. I wish I'd stayed in touch with my friends.
5. I wish I had let myself be happier.

Use these not as a warning - but as a guide.

Another quote my late friend Judy left me with:

"Tell me, what is it you plan to do
with your one wild and precious life?"

Mary Oliver

Please make time to explore the Six Fs. They really inspire clarity and deeper purpose.

About Sue Belton

Sue Belton is an award-winning leadership coach, strategist, and business mentor with over two decades of experience working with senior professionals in construction, finance, and professional services.

Known for her clarity, compassion, and straight-talking approach, she helps high achievers move from burnout to balance and reconnect with what matters most.

Her work goes beyond performance - it's about meaning, impact, and sustainable success. She is especially passionate about guiding leaders through personal and professional transitions, including the big one: how to plan the next chapter of life with purpose and intention.

With a background in business transformation and human behaviour, she brings both commercial acumen and emotional intelligence to every conversation. Whether working one-on-one or speaking on stage, her mission is clear: to help people shift from living on autopilot to leading - and living – on purpose.

www.suebelton.com

https://www.linkedin.com/in/suebelton/

Retire with Purpose: The Clarity Code for a Life You Choose

Vicki Wusche

Did anyone at school ever ask you, "What kind of life do you want?"

Probably not. From that moment on, every question became about your job, what you do and not what matters to you. It's as if society is designed to shape us into employees - rather than thinkers, creators or the architects of lives we want to live. Maybe you were too young to know the full answer… but imagine how differently you might feel if you were ever asked.

I have spoken to thousands of professionals and business owners about "What comes next after work?" and very few have an answer because we've never been asked before. Well, I am asking you now…

What would you do if you never had to work another day JUST to pay the bills?

Notice I haven't mentioned 'retire', because that word can overwhelm some people. Instead, I'm inviting you to consider the possibility that not needing to work, might bring you joy.

What if you could choose how you work, when and why?

Do you think you have been ignoring the concept of retirement because such a dramatic change feels overwhelming, on a financial or emotional level? Or perhaps you've never considered retirement because a life after work feels unimaginable? Either way, know you are not alone.

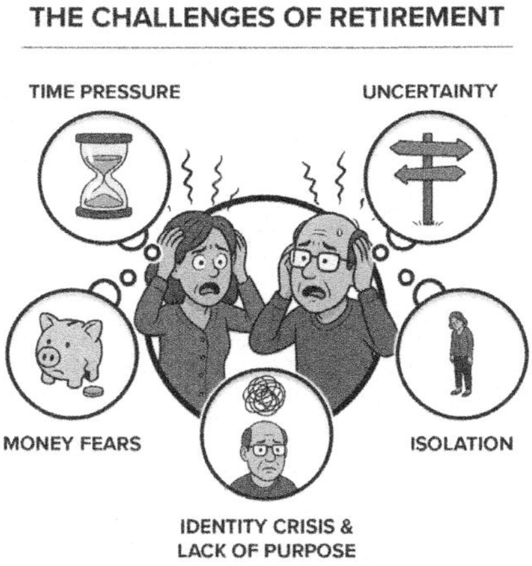

What if instead of focusing on 'retirement' we designed a life that you don't want to retire from? When I shared my thoughts around retirement in *Retire Inspire 1* - I had already created a process based on my personal experience of being made redundant (the other revolting R word).

Neither redundancy nor retirement sound inspiring or positive. They suggest being cast aside, a period of powerlessness, where someone decided you were no longer useful or because of your AGE! With a little preparation, you don't need to feel financially vulnerable or emotionally unprepared. More importantly, you don't need to feel pressured by a looming date.

Let's be clear, you are NOT alone in feeling this way. There is a way to navigate towards a life of your choosing 'A Wealthy Life'.

Your Wakeup Call

This 'change' is not about a lack of choice, it's about no one showing you that there is a path you can follow. Retirement began as a promise made by employers, to control employees working hard, in low-paid, physical jobs with the promise of a payout when they 'retire'.

In the UK, the Old Age Pension Act of 1909, set the retirement age at 70, despite the average life expectancy being between 44-48. Most employees never lived long enough to make a claim, that promise broken.

Fast forward to today and the retirement age in the UK is creeping up from 65 towards 70 again. Why? Because the Government can't afford to fund an ageing population living well into their 80s!

You need to understand that the real issue here is not just about the size of your pension pot. It's about the outdated belief that you need 'permission' to stop working. Who says you have to wait?

For vibrant, capable people – yes like you – it doesn't make sense to just completely stop work. You can and should design your own plan. To ease back from full time work, on your own terms, in your own time.

When I was made redundant from my university lecturer role, I had no financial cushion, no plan and no clarity. I'd like to tell you I bounced back quickly, but I didn't. I stumbled around trying to recreate the job that I loved. I even worked for free, which is of course unsustainable. I was 44 and on the 'scrap heap' (wherever that was!).

Over the next four years, I learned how to make my money work hard and independently of my time and then focused on what to do with all the extra time I had. I stepped into a new and constantly developing persona, one I frankly preferred.

I finally answered the question "What would I do if I never had to work again?"

Since then, I became one of *The Telegraph's Most Influential People in Property,* author of five best-selling books, contributor to another eight and I am the host of *A Wealthy Life* podcast which is approaching its 200th episode. I run a business helping clients understand and invest in property. I have three grandchildren, a huge greenhouse for my heritage tomatoes, lead a local climate action group, and when not scuba-diving, I cold-water swim five times a week. I also love my holidays.

My time is full of purpose and passion, my personal blend of means, memories, mission, multigenerational connections - more on that shortly.

This experience has enabled me to support other professionals and business owners to transition to 'A Wealthy Life'. Not as a retirement coach, but as someone who's lived the experience and knows that no matter what age you are now you can plan and live the life you want - 'A Wealthy Life'.

Working as a university lecturer I could never have imagined anything different. I can now and I love my life, 'A Wealthy Life' of my choosing, where I don't have to work to pay the bills, my passions lead the way.

The Clarity Code is a framework developed through personal and professional experience, mentoring clients over the last 15 years. It's designed to guide you through the perceived challenges of retirement and into a life of your own design.

5 STEPS TO A LIFE YOU CHOOSE

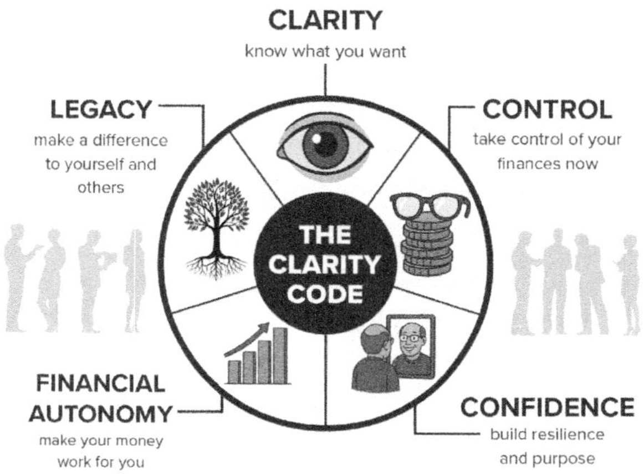

You can create the life you want, one filled with greater clarity, confidence and purpose, at any age, or stage of your career. However, you must ditch the word 'retirement' from your vocabulary. It's too small to describe the life you are about to imagine. If thinking about a life after work makes you feel uncomfortable, then just pause and allow your imagination to percolate on the possibilities.

Let me walk you through the five steps of the Clarity Code, each paired with a simple thought exercise to get you started.

No pressure here, we are just chatting. And remember I do this all the time so trust me.

1. Clarity – Permission To Imagine What's Possible

We need to uncover your 'why'. If you don't have a reason to plan your life beyond work, then we have already reached a FULL STOP.

Let me ask that question again in a different way…

Why would you stop working JUST to pay the bills?

It is a big question, think back to that careers interview (if you had one at school), when you were young and full of hope.

- Why did you want to be who you once dreamed of?
- Why do you love what you do now?
- Why do you wish you had more time or money and what's waiting for you?

You don't have to have all the answers, I know I didn't. This is about allowing yourself to imagine what's possible. Think of each new idea as a stepping stone. When you take the first step, then more steps will appear, ones you can't see until you move forwards.

Here's a couple of thought stepping stones for you...

- If you run a business, or work in corporate - do you want to start reducing your hours?
- Once you've taken a long holiday - then what do you want to do more of?

2. Control – Taking Charge Of Your Finances

Now that you've uncovered your 'why' it's time to understand 'what'.

Specifically, what have you got - financially speaking and how is it performing?

Most people I speak to can't confidently describe their financial position. Do you 'guesstimate' your budget, or are you a spreadsheet 'freak' like me? Do you actively monitor your finances and investments? Or like many people I speak to, are you simply trusting that your pension will be enough for your unplanned future?

Seriously, if you want to stop or simply reduce the time you spend earning money, then you need to know that you have 'enough' income to cover your essential bills and ideally 'more than enough' to enjoy life.

Financial control means:

- Knowing your monthly outgoings and lifestyle costs.
- Understanding where your money comes from and where it goes.
- Identifying underperforming assets.
- Having a dashboard (yes, it can be a spreadsheet).

Your thought stepping stones...

- Track your income and expenses as they are now. (There are resources available in The Wealthy Life Community link at the end of the chapter).
- If you had more free time, how would your expenses change and will you need more or less money moving forward?

3. Confidence – You Don't Need A Job Title To Feel Amazing

We have built a society that is tied to job titles. Our opening question to someone we meet is "What do you do?". Take away the title and you immediately lose status, structure, routine and sometimes even your own self-worth. You would still be you; your job title doesn't define your worth.

What if I had asked you "What matters to you most, what are you passionate about?"

Yes, a few people will include work.

I talk about this more in my fifth book *The Wealthy Retirement Plan*. I discussed redefining our time through four values-led categories:

- **Means** (how you generate income)
- **Memories** (what you cherish)
- **Mission** (what drives you), and
- **Multigenerational** (who you spend and share time with).

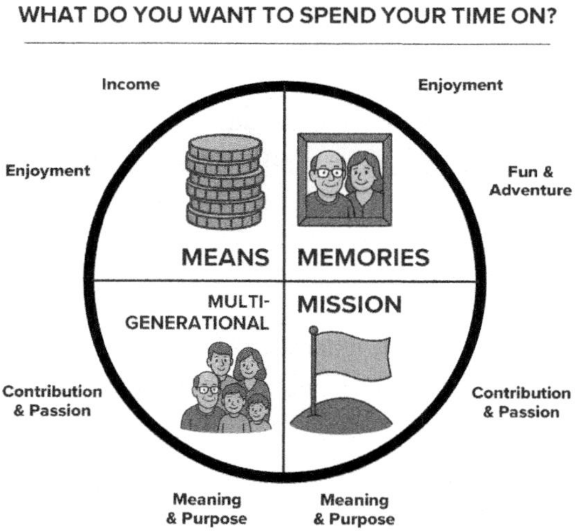

In summary: you can choose where you focus your time and energy.

I am passionate about helping people create lives full of the potential for amazingness! I love buying property investments for myself and clients, I love teaching people about money, sharing my knowledge about growing tomatoes, and the joys of cold-water swimming, but I don't have a job title!

Your thought stepping stones…

- What's your passion? Is it to be more artistic, protect the planet, nurture the next generation, finally bring that book to life, explore the world, serve your community or build something meaningful that leaves a legacy?

- What's the first step could you take towards doing more of what you love? Do you need more time, space or energy or simply a way to create income that doesn't rely on working to earn?

4. Financial Autonomy – Income That Works Without You

I speak to a lot of people who feel more financially vulnerable because of recent geo-political changes. We need to talk about personal financial autonomy not just financial security!

The solution is simple - know your numbers.

Having 'enough' money to cover six-months of your essential bills in an easy access, but high-rate savings account is a good start - a buffer. True financial autonomy means an income that isn't tied to your time.

Financial Autonomy means not relying on:

- The Government (who may change policies or age thresholds).
- Your employer (whose priorities can change).
- A pension (whose performance you can't guarantee).

Whether you have a state, employer or private pension, they are all based on stock market performance. That alone is not preparation enough for retirement.

For me, financial autonomy has come from property investment. Buying with mortgages to leverage capital, renting properties that produce profit, plus the potential of a capital gain just made perfect mathematical sense.

Let me share a basic example, but you don't need a million to start:

- 1 million in the bank at 4% interest = 40,000 per annum (nice, but is it enough and it's *not* guaranteed)
- 1 million leveraged into 16 small rental properties at 300/month net after costs = 4,800 per month, that's nearly 60,000 per annum after costs, plus potential capital growth.

Over time, those same houses will increase in capital or rental value. Then if you decide to reduce the portfolio to eight mortgage-free houses, it could generate over 75,000 per annum.

That's autonomy, efficient and independent. That's what I am focused on.

Your thought stepping stones...

- How much do you need to cover your basic expenses now and later in your life?
- How much income are you already generating independent of your time?

5. Legacy – What Mark Will You Leave On The World

This isn't about what you will leave in your will. Retirement is not an end, it's the 'how' you really want to live your life.

How do you want to spend your time and what impact do you want to make. Get the financial autonomy part right and your family will be fine - leaving you to spend what you want, guilt free!

This is about the legacy you could create while you're still here - with the time, energy, and wisdom you now have.

When you focus on contribution, and impact, sharing your skills to solve real-world problems, and inspire the next generation.

Imagine if all the brilliant and wonderful people like you, decided to put their heads together to solve the challenges we face in our communities, country and the planet?

Your thought stepping stones

- What are you passionate about? What's your mission or purpose? What do you get frustrated by and think there must be a better way?
- What group could you join or galvanise to leverage your skills and experience?
- And here's a third thought step - what insight or story could you share to inspire others?

Where Do You Go From Here?

I hope that I have inspired you to think differently. If you're wondering, "Where do I start?" I'd love to offer you a free 30-minute call with me. I promise: the possibilities people uncover in these conversations are always extra-ordinary.

If you've read this far and you are feeling some regret, I hear you. So many of the people I speak to say, "I wish I'd done this years ago." And here's the harsh truth:

You can't start earlier. But you can start now.

Ooh, did you feel that?

That ripple of anticipation, maybe a little excitement and a sprinkle of nerves. That visceral shift was your intuition letting you know something needs to change - and yes it can.

This can be the moment that changes everything. Are you ready to:

- Stop wondering and start planning?
- Understand your finances with confidence?
- Create a retirement - a life on your terms – 'A Wealthy Life'?

Why not take an easy first step; book a free call with me now: *bit.ly/BookVicki*

You bring the trickle of possibilities, and I'll help you build the plan. Let's retire on purpose, on our terms, following our passions towards a truly Wealthy Life.

About Vicki Wusche

Transitioning from redundancy to a Non-Traditional Retirement, in four years, gave Vicki Wusche a unique insight into the importance of financial autonomy and the freedom to choose how your time is spent.

In her number one Amazon best-selling fifth book, *'The Wealthy Retirement - A revolutionary guide to living the rest of your life in style'*, she explains how you can also stop working to pay the bills and start living the rest of your life the way you choose.

Her podcast *A Wealthy Life* is a blend of financial mindset, inspiration and property investment stories, because property investment gives Vicki and her clients, financial autonomy.

When not writing books, speaking, buying property, swimming or on holiday, Vicki enables her clients to create their ideal retirement, by identifying resources, leveraging them appropriately and developing the Wealthy Life they want to live for many years to come.

Vicki@Wusche-Associates.co.uk

Or connect on all the normal social channels as there is just one Vicki Wusche.

Book a complimentary call with Vicki *https://bit.ly/BookVicki*

Listen to A Wealthy Life Podcast on iTunes or Spotify

Watch her inspirational video on the need for female financial resilience, The Smart Woman's Ultimate Guide to Money and Investing *Https://bit.ly/Smart-WUG*

Join The Wealthy Life Community (full of resources) for free *Https://bit.ly/Join-WLC*

Hybrid Retirement – The Best Of Both Worlds

Chris Beesley And Susan Beesley

"Conventional Retirement" Doesn't Work Anymore!"

In Today's World "Retirement" Is About Waking Up To Your New Way Of Life…Your Life…Your Second Act

What Is Retirement Today?

Forget everything you think you know about retirement.

The rules have changed.

Many people still rely on the old ways of saving and investing, but here's the problem: that's just not enough anymore.

"Conventional retirement" is all about getting to a certain age and stopping work. It is all about the money…

How much have you got in your pension pot?

How much income will you have?

Will you have to downsize?

Will you run out of money?

Many retirement planners still have it the wrong way round... how much money do you have, now let's see how you can retire!

But today that has all changed...

Retirement is not just about money...it's waking up to a new way of life...your life...your second act.

We believe that today your retirement planning should be...

#1. What do I want to do in retirement? and #2. How can I make it happen?

We call it a **Hybrid Retirement** and it's going to last 20 to 30 years or more.

Now maybe you've never heard of *Hybrid Retirement.*

In today's world retirement is now what you make it.

It's no longer a one-size fits all time of life.

We believe retirement is not a destination marked by a stop sign—it's a continuation of life, a new chapter filled with energy, purpose, and potential.

In a nutshell, Hybrid Retirement is a combination of work, leisure and freedom activities allowing you the flexibility to enjoy your new chapter of life.

And flexibility is a key word because you never know what curveballs life will throw at you in your mid-sixties.

In 2019 Susan's mum developed dementia and needed help and looking after. We became her full-time carers.

Our challenge was she lived an hour and a half away and she didn't want to live with us...driving three hours every day around the M25 was not a sustainable option.

We had to make a new plan.

We sold our house and moved close to Susan's mum in February 2020, just before the pandemic lockdown.

Our carer's role lasted two and a half years.

Something that had we still had our traditional accounting and consulting business would have been virtually impossible.

So with a *Hybrid Retirement* we look at things differently.

Because now in the 21st century when governments want to reduce their social security costs, continue to increase the retirement age at which you can draw your pension and investment returns are volatile you need to take matters into your own hands.

It's a way you can combine all the traditional aspects of retirement with part-time work, what we call "Work a little; Live a lot".

Part-time work can be new entrepreneurial ventures or passion projects you might have been considering but never had the time for allowing you to stay mentally engaged, financially secure and fulfilled... a life where you no longer have to choose between working or retiring but rather a retirement you design to balance financial wellness and mental wellness.

Today where our life expectancy is way longer we have this incredible gift of time and many years to enjoy life but also remain connected to your skills, your income and your sense of purpose... and it will be different for everyone.

Our belief is that today you need five pillars for a successful retirement and everyone can have them if you're prepared to change your way of thinking.

#1. Financial Security With A Residual Income Not Financial Stress

The last thing any of us want in "retirement" is financial stress because we haven't for whatever reason been able to save or create a big enough pension pot to provide sufficient income for us to live the life we want to live.

In our chapter in Retire Inspire 1 we introduced you to our 21st Century 3 Legged Stool...

"A New Way Of Thinking And Funding Your Retirement"

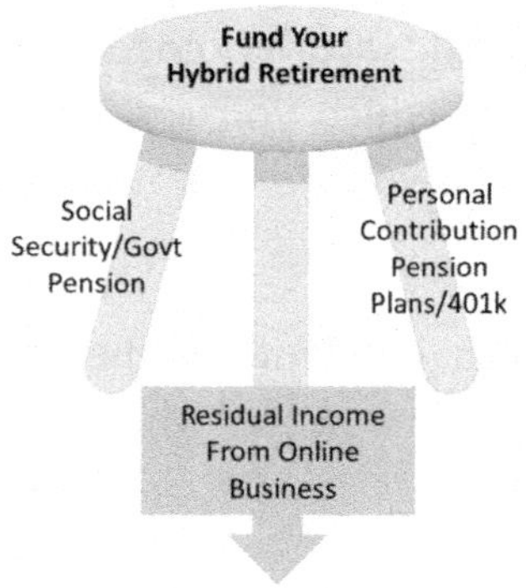

And that model has stood the test of time...it's as strong today as it was back in 2019.

Having a way of creating income from your online business that is totally under your control is essential.

#2. Have A Sense Of Purpose... An Exciting Reason To Get Up In The Morning

Can you imagine not having anything to do...the thought absolutely horrifies us and probably does you too?

Recently we had a conversation with Sally - she's a 60 year old woman whose husband works away during the week and she is the carer for her 90 year old father.

He has just gone into day care for three days a week so she now has plenty of spare time on her hands and has absolutely nothing to do.

During our conversation it emerged that she wanted to learn a new skill and create an income of £2,000 per month that she would save as an additional nest-egg for her retirement.

She decided to join our community, learn affiliate marketing and start building a monthly residual income.

She's excited to be doing something new and that gives her a purpose in life.

#3. Remain Active – Do Those Things You've Always Wanted To Do When You Had The Time, To Travel And Have Life Experiences

"Once the travel bug bites there is no known antidote, and I know I shall be happily infected until the end of my life"
Michael Palin

We all have a bucket list, those things we want to see and do "once we have the time" and it's really important that you do them.

They keep you active, they give you things to plan for and look forward to achieving.

And if you have the travel bug like we do you're always asking "where shall we go next?"

And age should not be a barrier!

We've swam with dolphins in Mexico, we've jumped off a mountain with a parachute in the French Alps, we've zip lined in the Caribbean, we've ridden horses on the beach at sunset in Costa Rica, we've kayaked in the mangroves in Curacao.

We're not saying this to boast but to inspire you because they're all experiences we've had after age 60!

Don't be one of those people who looks back on their life and regret something they didn't do.

#4. Keep Mentally And Physically Healthy

We confess we really didn't take too much notice of this as we've stayed pretty active playing badminton (how we met) and we been skiers since 1991.

But sometimes life throws you curve balls and you find you need to do more to stay physically healthy as you get a little older (yes it happened to us with a health wake-up call round about the time of the pandemic).

Today we walk most days, we have some essentia[illegible] equipment on our terrace and since moving to Spain we're looking to take up pickle ball.

It's also important to keep the brain active, which for us is our online business which keeps us using our brain and now we're learning Spanish.

It really is super important to pay attention to your physical and mental health!

#5. Stay Relevant And Connected, Be Socially Active And Be Part Of An Inspiring Community

During your "work" years you build up a community of like-minded people and over time it changes.

But you always have people around you who inspire you and you can turn to when the need arises.

Once you leave the work environment your community slowly starts to dwindle because you no longer have things in common.

It is therefore essential to become part of a community that will take you into retirement before you get there.

When we started our online journey which was before we "retired" our traditional business we became part of an online community of people who were prepared to inspire, help and guide us as we learnt and implemented new skills.

Today, 15 years later we are still part of that online community, giving back more than we take by helping "newbies" and in addition we meet up physically at least once a year normally in a lovely location.

ed to Spain we've made the effort to become
community, even joining a walking/hiking group
e of the amazing places where we live because
sn't a reason not to!

The thing about building these five pillars is that you can start to build them before you retire so when the time comes the switch over is seamless.

So *Hybrid Retirement* is a combination of work, leisure and freedom.

The leisure and freedom aspects are a matter of personal choice but what about work?

Here's our thoughts on some ideas that might suit you…

#1. Part-Time Work

This is one of the most popular forms of hybrid retirement plan because you can work a few days or a few hours a week whatever suits you.

It provides a steady income, the all-important community and a sense of purpose.

The potential downside is that you are still working for somebody else and so have to ask for time off if you want to travel and secondly you are not location free.

#2. Consulting Or Coaching

If you have some specialised skills, knowledge or expertise you may want to consider consulting or coaching as it allows you to work on your own terms and the income potential could be significant.

People across the world are searching for information and education every single day and your life experiences, knowledge and skills are all incredibly valuable assets that you can share.

It's a flexible and rewarding way to continue working while enjoying your life at the same time.

The downside again is that you are at the beck and call of your clients and may not have location freedom.

A solution maybe to coach or consult online.

This is something Susan does working with women over 50.

#3. Starting A Business

Today this is probably the most popular hybrid strategy and in particular because of the internet.

Robert Laura, author of *The Naked Retirement* said in an article in Forbes magazine.

"I believe the concept of starting a business for retirement income will become one of the most significant trends impacting retirement in the 21st century...That means helping people find ways to turn a passion, hobby, or personal desire into extra money in their pocket...not to mention helping people see the importance of planning for the non-financial aspects of retirement such as replacing a work identity, staying relevant and connected, as well as keeping mentally and physically fit."

With your own business the potential for growth is limitless and is a great way to stay engaged and active while providing a source of income totally under your control.

If we add to that the internet, so your business is an online business, you now have a global customer base, the ability to work from anywhere and automation will allow your business to grow whilst you are enjoying your leisure activities.

For us this is the best hybrid strategy because when you choose the right business model it gives you financial freedom, location freedom and time freedom.

As well as the ability to help others live their best life.

There are many options for starting an online business and it's important to do your research and find the right one for your circumstances.

Today, we live an active life in Spain, we've had an online business for 15 years that we started in our mid-fifties, we travel, we spend time doing the things we love with people we love and help, guide and inspire others to live their dream retirement lifestyle whatever that is for them.

The Hybrid Retirement has worked for us and we know it can work for you too.

If you want to remain active, have a sense of purpose, be financially secure for your "retirement" years and have a life of freedom without having to rely on others a hybrid retirement strategy maybe the perfect solution for you.

We stopped by to stir your soul – make sure to enjoy the best years of your life

About Chris Beesley and Susan Beesley

Chris and Susan Beesley are former accountants and management consultants now living their version of retirement in Spain. Their wake-up call came in their mid-50s when, after a lifetime of self-employment, they realised their traditional pension provisions were lacking. Faced with advice that they'd need over £1 million to retire comfortably, they turned to property investing—until the 2008 financial crash forced a rethink.

Instead of going back to corporate life, they built a six-figure online education business, using their professional expertise to help others transition into online entrepreneurship. Now in their 70s, they coach and mentor clients worldwide and speak on global stages about modern retirement and second-act careers.

Chris and Susan are authors of several books on creating retirement income the 21st-century way and host the award-winning podcast *Living The Retirement Lifestyle*. They are passionate advocates for mental wellness, staying active, and living retirement with purpose and possibility.

Website: https://ChrisAndSusanBeesley.com

Podcast: *https://LivingTheRetirementLifestyle.com*

https://Facebook.com/ChrisAndSusanBeesley

https://Instagram.com/SusanAndChris

If Not Now, *When*? Finances, Fun, And Freedom In Retirement And Life

Anne Taylor

This topic is close to my heart. I turned 60 this year and can say, unequivocally, that finances and retirement have been themes I have learned, lived, and long championed for almost 40 years - initially blindly, and later with clarity and purpose.

I'm passionate about this for two reasons: one emotional, one practical.

The Emotional Connection

This is the topic that most connects me to my Dad. Some of my most vivid memories of him involve financial lessons - overt and covert. These moments were rare and intimate. Our strongest connections were cerebral, not emotional. Finances and freedom (more on that later) were the few things he discussed directly with me that, on reflection, didn't involve me proving myself. I soaked up those lessons because they were wrapped in the kind of attention I craved.

That attention, although infrequent, planted seeds of deep awareness. I didn't fully realize it at the time, however, each time we had those talks, or I noticed his behaviour and off-handed comments, I was learning how to think, prioritize, and take responsibility. These were values that shaped me.

The Practical Impact

I was fortunate to learn about personal finances early. Initially I followed my Dad's advice without fully understanding it. Over time, I got informed and built financial habits that continue to serve me. In hindsight, I can see how these practices gave me a strong foundation that many others, especially women, didn't receive.

Curiously, my Mum didn't feature in any of these financial teachings. As an adult, I realized that many women - friends, colleagues, clients, even fellow coaches - didn't know their own financial picture. This is still the case. The data backs this up (accurate at time of publishing):

- Globally, women earn about 77 cents for every 'dollar' earned by men (ILO, UN Women).
- Women's pensions are 30–40% lower than men's across the EU, similar in the U.S. (World Economic Forum).
- Women often score lower on financial literacy tests, particularly in investing and retirement planning (FINRA, OECD).

My parents died 20 years ago and every day I feel gratitude to them for my Dad's financial lessons and their example.

Lessons from Dad: My Early Financial Education

Here are some of the key lessons my Dad taught me in no particular order:

1. Budgeting is Thinking, Not Perfection

The most vivid memory I have was sitting with my Dad who showed me how to do a budget in my teens. He sat down with a paper and pencil writing the following list:

Item	Amount/Cost
Rent/Housing	
Tuition	
Food	
Toiletries	
Transportation	
TV/Cable	
Utilities (Water, gas, energy)	
Books	
School supplies	
Social activities	
Clothing	
Holidays	
Miscellaneous	

He asked me to estimate the annual costs. His goal wasn't accuracy - it was thinking and learning the process. Think before you spend. Understand what you need. Plan. I was learning how to anticipate needs, the breadth of those needs and to assign value. Think through all your needs, not just wants.

2. Spend Less Than You Earn

Which was the ultimate point of the budget exercise.

Live beneath your means. This became a lifelong habit. I had several part-time jobs through my tweens and teens - cooking, babysitting and retail jobs. Even in adulthood I baked custom cakes for colleagues and friends while working full-time. These were all things I enjoyed and didn't do for the money although they brought in income. I tracked spending. Today I periodically ask: *Do I need all these streaming services? Can my broadband provider match a better offer? Where are savings possible?*

At work, goals are set, tracked and adjusted. You need personal financial targets too. Living beneath your means becomes liberating, not restrictive. You create a cushion hence reducing worry of the unexpected. You often become more mindful of what brings joy, beyond purchasing. It gives you the motivation to say no, not trying to compete with others. It's not sacrifice, it's strategic empowerment. Know your numbers – income and expenses.

3. You Are Smart Enough To Handle Your Money

My Dad taught me this through his trust and (high) expectation. When I suggested applying for a scholarship where he worked, he said, "No. You'll fund yourself, and if you can't, we will assist you. Let someone else who needs it benefit from that scholarship." His belief: take ownership because you're smart and capable. That was empowering, and it also felt solitary and heavy. I learned to rely on myself. That self-reliance helped me become resilient, however, in contrast, it has taken time to learn how to ask for help when needed. Learn about money, you are resourceful enough to ask for help.

4. Start Early, Or At Least Now

When I was 18, I opened a small retirement account at a bank down the road from my university because I saw an ad in the window. I didn't fully "know" what I was doing. I remembered Dad saying you can't rely on the government or an employer pension. Today, that tiny investment is worth 24 times more. If you're reading this later in life, start now, it's better than never. The Rule of 72 says that on average money invested can double in seven years. Compounding is powerful. Small actions taken early become massive advantages later.

5. Money Buys Freedom

My Dad retired early by choice when I graduated high school. New management came in where he worked, and he didn't like the direction it took. Since he had planned for decades, he could walk away. That's financial freedom. Retirement isn't just about stopping work - it's about choosing how to live.

6. Wealth Is Different Than Income

Dad tracked investments on graph paper. I watched. Saving and investing created wealth. High income means little if it all gets spent. I often say, "buying something on sale, doesn't make it a deal if you don't actually need it." It's not what you make; it's what you keep and grow.

Dad's lessons weren't all easy. Being raised to be fiercely independent came with trade-offs. Having to save, pay my own way, not expect a partner, government or company to help can be empowering in one sense and isolating in another. Assets create options, investigate all avenues.

Financial Partnership: Building Together

Fast forward a couple of years to when I met my now ex-husband who had a negative net worth – not as drastic as it sounds, his car was worth more than the car loan. He had never learned these lessons.

A chance meeting with a financial planner at a friend's wedding changed things. That planner became a guide and partner.

We worked together:

1. Start by Identifying Your Life Goals

It's not money for money's sake. It's about creating the freedom to live your values. That's where the fun comes in. We asked: What matters to us? How do we want to live in 5, 10, 20 years? Those answers shaped our financial plan.

2. Spend Where It Matters

What you value shows in your bank account and your calendar by how you spend your money and time. We bought a small house outside the city. It met two of our goals: home ownership and early retirement. Our choices reflected our goals. People didn't always understand, yet we knew we were investing in freedom.

3. Live While You Plan

We did enjoy our lives while working our plan - Life is for living. We always had a holiday and a social fund. We didn't feel deprived. Now as a coach I realize we lived with an abundance mindset: belief that we could improve our financial position over time. Scarcity is the opposite: fear and limitation. Our abundance mindset meant we made decisions from optimism, not fear.

4. Play the Long Game

My ex was a spender; I was a saver. He paid all the bills he could. I invested a regular amount monthly. We adjusted contributions as our income grew. After a while we didn't notice it going out. We tracked our net worth (assets minus liabilities, hopefully positive). We didn't micromanage. We planned for the long term and ignored daily market noise. Long-term vision allows you to breathe, even when markets are turbulent.

5. Consider A Financial Planner

Ours educated, motivated, and held us accountable. He prompted us to do things we might have delayed - like wills and powers of attorney (POA). Since we were talking about goals and money, estate planning was a natural next step. He made financial discussions feel empowering, not intimidating.

Plan For The Unexpected

Fast forward to my parents' deaths, unexpectedly 22 weeks apart, I learned even more. My brother and I navigated probate and estate closures. That experience solidified an emerging idea I'd had.

Be Organized.

I had started a *"Life and Death Binder."* It contained my will, POAs, and national insurance number.

When I moved to Switzerland it required the next level of organization as worldwide wealth was also taxed necessitating disclosure of global assets (eg Canadian bank accounts). Another move to the UK further grew the binder to include property information, bank statements, a copy of every bank card, pension details, passport, driver's license and my advisor's contact details.

If you've ever had to close an estate, you know how many people and institutions need to be informed. I was sad about how my parents' lives were reduced to an administrative exercise externally. I learned things change over time, even without moving, so I revisit it annually now to ensure it's up to date. Writing this chapter has prompted me to add a secure list of my digital accounts and passwords to the binder.

So, Where's The Fun?

We aren't defined by our resume/curriculum vitae – as much as we work. We are so much more than that. The fun is in discovering and living our full selves. That's especially important before retirement. You don't want to be working 8-10 hours one day and home with idle time the next.

It's in the dreaming, planning, choosing. It's in having an abundance mindset. It's in living aligned to your goals. For me, a planner, I enjoy the process as well. Fun is found in whatever brings you joy - for me that's singing, Pilates, hiking, cooking, choir, learning, giving.

Fun is also knowing your future isn't limited. When you've set the stage financially, your options expand. And fun isn't just about big vacations or expensive hobbies. It's about the freedom to say yes. To rest. To be curious. To be passionate. To pivot.

Find The Fun For You.

Right now, my fun is a personal project I call my *"60-4-60 Quest"* - 60 experiences with others between my 60th and 61st birthdays. It's included hiking Scafell Pike (England's tallest peak), visiting a specialty food store, eating s'mores over an open fire (chocolate, biscuit, marshmallow campfire treats), seeing a play, axe throwing and stand-up paddle boarding so far.

And it doesn't have to be expensive.

Your Turn: Reflect And Plan

I've been lucky to start early. I'm grateful for the early lessons and example. I live a life now that blends part-time executive coaching with nature walks, travel, and community. My habits gave me the flexibility to design a life I love.

What would make your retirement fun?

What would make finances and the planning process more enjoyable?

What are the goals you've postponed because you thought you couldn't afford them?

What mindset do you hold about money? Scarcity or abundance?

What are your earliest memories about finances, and how have they shaped your habits?

What legacy do you want to leave - financially, emotionally, practically?

If you haven't started: identify your goals, know your numbers (income and expenses), create a plan, and begin putting something away every month. Even Now. And do things that bring you joy daily.

If not you, *who*?

If not now, *when*?

About Anne Taylor

Anne Taylor believes real success isn't just what you achieve – it's how you live. After more than 25 years in senior leadership roles with global Fortune 500 companies across North America and Europe, Anne made a deliberate shift from corporate life to coaching, helping high-achieving leaders grow beyond technical expertise into confident, people-focused leadership.

Now an ICF-certified executive and leadership coach, speaker, and award-winning author of *Soft Skills* **HARD RESULTS**, Anne blends sharp business insight with emotional intelligence. Her book reflects her own journey – learning to lead with both head and heart. In *Retire Inspire 2*, Anne shares powerful financial lessons shaped by her father's wisdom and her own life experience. Her story goes beyond money – it's about freedom, fulfillment, and living intentionally.

Anne now helps others navigate their next chapter with clarity and courage. She lives by the ninth principle of her book: *Live a Life of No Regrets.*

Website: *https://directions-coaching.com/*

Book: *https://mybook.to/SoftSkillsHardResults*

Contact me: *https://directions-coaching.com/contact/*

LinkedIn: *https://www.linkedin.com/in/anne-taylor-6b2a8311/*

Insta: *https://www.instagram.com/annetaylorcoach/*

I Failed Retirement And This is what I Discovered

Carol A Vincie

When I joined the corporate workforce in the mid-1960s, the goal was to be hired by a large organization and retire from that same company.

I had the opportunity to work on an assignment that shattered my long term beliefs that the brokerage industry abided by the rules intended to protect securities when left in their possession. While working on this assignment, I was able to observe the impact of the Cuban crisis as these immigrants were hired in this industry with little knowledge of the English language – match on color was the way many certificates where stored.

My next assignment gave me the opportunity to work on a plan for improving the US health care system. This put me in Chicago for four months while traveling throughout the county to interview various Blue Cross/Blue Shield locations. I just got off a plane in Providence, RI where I learned about the Olympic massacre in Munich. This assignment gave my sister the chance to use my apartment in Manhattan. She complained that this was the only assignment I had worked on that finished on time which took her back to our parents' home. The election of a republican president put this project on hold and the US health care system continues to suffer from the failure to implement our suggestions

I progressed with much effort to advance into what were considered non-traditional positions for women – sales, sales management, and Executive Briefing centers. During the 1980s, large organizations where required to report the number of women in key management positions.

I was the highest-ranking woman on the Poughkeepsie manufacturing site with 15,000 employees when my manager recognized that I was bored. He suggested we find my next career move. The site manager complained that if I left that would screw up his EEOC numbers. The quality of the relationship with that manager was reflected in him sharing that feedback and my response.

My next significant career move was an assignment supporting PCs in the Far East, Central and South America. This was another position where women were not welcomed. Anticipating regular trips to Tokyo, I registered for Japanese classes at a local university. This allowed me to start my first presentation in Tokyo with a few opening statements in Japanese.

When I returned from this assignment, my career manager suggested I list all my first- and second-line managers. He stated "You cannot push a rope into the executive level. You need to find a prior manager who can pull you into those positions". This list revealed that 80% of my prior managers were no longer in the organization. The company we joined no longer existed. This was a message I failed to recognize until after I took advantage of an early retirement program.

I had carefully selected the people I worked for who would accept my ADD – Attention Deficit Disorder, undiagnosed – work style. I worked on two more challenging and significant projects. One with a major US retail organization that required coordination with hardware and software development operations throughout the US and Europe.

The last assignment was a report to the Corporate Management Committee (CMC) where I was the client contact to understand why a range of clients were abandoning the cash cow of the organization for the small, under-utilized computing units that were the forerunner of what we all now carry in our pockets.

Without the support of a prior manager, I was labeled subversive, and retirement was the only option.

I played tennis almost every day. I worked on some major landscaping projects at my home. I was so busy and wondered how I managed to fit work into my prior 25 years.

After two months, I was BORED!!! I reveled in problem solving when others had given up and declared there was no solution. Not yet 50, the corporate world was imploding. I had guessed right in my choice of an organization to work for where their growth provided as many challenges as I could absorb. Where was I going to find another playground for my creativity, my boundless energy, and my visionary skills?

I discovered the Venture Capital (VC) arena. I grew up in a working-class household. Every time I announced I had a new job in my organization, my dad asked, "What was wrong with the last one?" I studied Economics as a minor in college, so the issues in VC were not completely unfamiliar.

The VC world was the ideal fit for my ADD brain. The creativity, energy, and self-belief of these individuals betting everything on their products reminded me of my corporate experiences.

Without an MBA, and my hair turning grey early, gramma was telling these 20 something guys how to run their businesses. I needed a hook. What could I offer to get their attention? I provided assessments for their staff as a free service. This gave me insights into significant holes in their staffing that might repel investors.

This technique got me a client. I had experience with the product they were repackaging. During my corporate days, I hired a number of people in a number of roles. The five people they had on staff were not going to attract any investment capital. Spent my first 90 days on the project hiring 41 people. Those were a minimum of 12-hour days to complete the assessment reviews, interviews, and offers. Good talent did not stay on the market for even a week during this period. The last person I hired was the HR Director. I have continued to use the same assessment products for over a quarter of a century.

I continued to work with this client through the S-4 submission process to the Securities and Exchange Commission (SEC) and finding a $15M investor. There was never an agreement on the evaluation of the company.

The VC arena collapsed in April, 2000. My $7M in stock became wallpaper. This was the next time I was faced with retirement.

Returning to the question – Where can I find a field that provides the challenge, inspiration, and quality of people that will consume all my energy???

During my corporate days and the requirements to move for promotions, I had maintained an inventory of real estate properties. The downturns of 1991 and 2008 whipped out those investments and lacked the criteria to satisfy the items listed above.

There is also temporary retirement. This probably impacts women more than our male colleagues. If you are part of the sandwich generation, dealing with kids and parents. There are times when they demand all our attention. I do not have children and at the time my only sibling was living an airplane ride away, so I was it.

Both my parents passed with Dementia. I was not aware of the signs and symptoms when my dad was developing the condition. My mom would not allow a care giver in their home, so I was partially involved. After he passed, she then started showing the signs. Since I was not involved with my dad's progression with the condition, I was not able to spot the signs until I was called by the police at midnight after having an extremely difficult day to retrieve her at a hospital that was two hours away from my home.

I took my mom into my home for four years. Her symptoms included not being able to tell day from night and would attempt to leave the house several times during the night. This required large bells on all the doors so I would wake up to continue the argument that it was not time to go to the center. I was fortunate to find a senior center with excellent services. This allowed me to get six hours of time for grocery shopping, car repairs, and a round of golf each week. I had to completely curtail my businesses during this period. Eventually, she had to be put into a facility. Even this was a challenge. She used all the skills that got her through the challenges of living through the depression but made her an unacceptable patient at many facilities.

I did not get the retirement gene. I have found the activity that will take me through to my expiration date.

I have referenced my undiagnosed ADD – Attention Deficit

Disorder. 10 years ago, I found a label for the condition I have struggled with for my entire life. I was at a seminar at UBS. I was on the email list for one of the speakers. The senior executives at UBS invited three extremely ADHD males to speak to his management team. He introduced the session with these comments.

You need to listen carefully to the comment of these three extremely successful men. One is a medical doctor, one a speaker on ADHD getting $25,000 for his presentations, one an entrepreneur. You have people on your staff who will not conform to traditional corporate behaviors. If you do not treat them appropriately, they will leave, go to work for our competition and we will never catch up.

This is extremely powerful insight that many more managers and business owners need to reflect.

As I sat in the audience, I was able to relate to the many strengths and symptoms of ADD/ADHD. Yet despite all the challenges I jumped into during my corporate days, I was not able to even whisper to my close friends that I was ADD for five years. This included two years with a coach who encouraged me to recognize that ADD is my unique selling proposition.

Now I am an outspoken voice for the Strengths and Powers of the condition. I am awaiting the release date for my book – A Parent's Guide to Supporting Your ADD/ADHD Daughter. I am creating 7-card decks that address the Symptoms, Strengths, and Struggles for these individuals: Entrepreneurs, Employers, Employees, Educators, Empowers, Empaths, and Elders. These will be found on Deckible.com/ADHD and in physical card decks.

Retirement takes many forms. If you had to take on the "family business", this could be the time to follow your passion. If family responsibilities required you to take on roles that were not your choice, take advantage of the value of age and experience in volunteer activities. If you choose the military, police or firefighter, these roles provide retirement benefits when you are still young enough to start again.

The key to your remaining years is to review your skills, experiences, passions to make yourself an inspiring and fun person to be around.

I retain my competitive spirit, and my golf tee times are as serious an event as my speaking engagements.

Best wishes for your retirement!

About Carol Vincie

Carol Vincie took many, many decades to understand that her creativity, drive, and high energy, had a name – Attention Deficit Disorder (ADD).

As she looked back over her life:

- Starting her first business at 16 with no concern about failing. This was quite unusual at the time.
- Recognizing there were assignments she could never successfully complete even if her life depended on it.
- Being selective in managers would accept her unique work style and having the courage to walk away when it was not a good fit.These are all behaviors she encourages everyone to model with or without ADD or ADHD.

As her titles says – *I Failed Retirement,* provides her the opportunity to use her skills acquired over a lifetime to slow her aging process, engage with communities to avoid isolation, while leaving time for her favorite leagure activity - golf.

Carol will continue speaking up and speak out until that unknown expiration date.

CarolVincie@gmail.com

\

Retirement Wasn't for Me, So I Created Something Better

Andrew Middleton

I didn't retire. There was no party. No farewell cake. No speech with polite applause.

No one handed me a brochure with *"Next Steps"* printed on the cover. At 58, I simply paused. After a long career filled with leadership roles, creative projects, and big conversations, I found myself stepping back. Not out of failure, not out of fear, but because something in me said, this chapter is done.

I didn't know what came next. I just knew it wouldn't be a traditional retirement. I wasn't finished. I wasn't ready for beige cardigans and cruise catalogues.

I also wasn't prepared for what came instead. It started quietly, as these things often do. A colleague made a joke about "having one eye on the exit." Someone else asked, "Have you thought about winding down?" It wasn't cruel. Just casual, almost caring.

But it landed like a stone in my stomach. That was the moment I realised I had entered what I now call the dangerous decade. It's the stretch of time from your mid-fifties to mid-sixties when the world starts to look at you differently. Not with admiration or interest, but with an awkward kind of pity.

Ageism begins to creep in. People assume you've peaked. Opportunities become harder to find. The invitations slow down.

The phone doesn't ring quite as often. You haven't changed, but the way others see you has. One day you're experienced. The next, you're seen as expensive, out of date, or simply not worth considering.

It's not always obvious. It's not always intentional. But it's real. I wasn't fading.

But it felt like the world had already decided I should be.

So I made a choice. I stepped away before someone else made the decision for me. With full-time work behind me, I did what many mid-lifers do when no one is hiring but you're not ready to stop.

I became a consultant. Which, if we're being honest, is a polite way of saying I made a website, joined too many Zoom calls, and started charging day rates based on the project vibe. I told people I had a *portfolio* career. That sounds slick, but really it just means I was absolutely winging it.

One week I was coaching a CEO. The next I was helping a charity sort out its messaging. Then I was making a PowerPoint for a man named Darren who paid me in Greggs vouchers. I tried everything.

Webinars. Mentoring. Interim roles. Podcasting.

At one point, I ran a pop-up think tank. Another time, I found myself hosting a corporate improv session. That's when I learned to be more careful with the word "yes." Some of it was fascinating. Some of it was nonsense.

All of it was useful. This wasn't retirement. But it wasn't a traditional career either. It was something else.

I just didn't have the words for it yet.

I didn't jump from full-time work into a dream role. I didn't sell everything and move to a Greek island. I didn't go back to school or start a business.

I drifted. Lightly. Gently. Honestly.

At first, I thought I was just filling the space. But slowly, I realised I was creating something new. Something flexible, purposeful, and deeply satisfying. I wasn't disappearing.

I was redefining. As I spoke with others in the same boat, people who had left full-time work but still had projects, passion, and plenty to offer, I began describing what we were doing as a kind of soft retirement. And that phrase stuck.

Soft retirement became my way of describing a new phase of life. Not full-time, not finished. Not slowing down completely, but choosing your own pace. A way of staying curious, useful, and involved without handing over your whole week.

No one had called it that before. But as soon as I said it, people nodded. That's exactly what I am doing, they'd say. I just didn't know it had a name.

Now it does.

Soft retirement is not a weaker version of your old career. It is not a fallback plan. It is not retirement-lite.

It is a new chapter. Designed by you. You still work, but it is work that fits your values and energy. You contribute, but not out of obligation. You explore, reflect, and make space for what matters.

Where hard retirement feels like a full stop, soft retirement is more like a comma. A pause. A shift in direction. Not an end.

You are not exiting the world. You are entering it differently.

My week doesn't run on the old Monday to Friday schedule anymore. And that is exactly how I like it.

I have a paid role that sometimes involves weekend work, and I build the rest of my time around that. It is work I enjoy and believe in, and it fits well with how I live now.

Midweek, I might take time out with my wife. We go for a walk, explore somewhere new, or just sit and have a proper conversation. I don't wait for permission to enjoy the day. I just make space for it.

Wherever I am, I run a membership community I created called INDY. It stands for *I'm Not Done Yet.* It's a space for people navigating soft retirement. Still active. Still working in their own way. Still full of ideas and purpose.

I invented the term INDYs to describe us, independent, inspired, involved people who are not quite retired, but not living by the old rules either.

We've moved beyond job titles, but we haven't lost our sense of contribution. Some of us are working part-time, freelancing, volunteering, mentoring, starting new ventures, or simply exploring life on our own terms. We're curious, committed, and carving out a space between full-time work and full-time rest.

And here's the unexpected part. That flexible lifestyle I used to see in influencer posts or odd online ads, the ones promising freedom through digital nomad life has quietly become my reality. Earlier this year, I found myself answering emails in Belize.

No hype. No big announcement. Just the freedom to work where I am, stay connected to a vibrant community, and shape my time around what matters.

Looking back, one of the hardest parts wasn't adjusting to slower mornings or a changing income. It was letting go of identity. For years, I had introduced myself by my job title. Without it, I had to figure out who I was again. It's not easy. When you've spent decades being a "something," learning to just be yourself takes time.

But that's where soft retirement shines. It gives you room to find out who you are underneath all the roles and labels. You realise that your value was never in the title, it was in how you showed up and what you brought to the table.

I remember a turning point early in this journey. A friend asked me to host a small community event. It wasn't a big deal. It didn't pay much. But I said yes. That day, standing in front of a thoughtful group of people, something shifted. I wasn't there to impress or prove anything. I was just there to help. It felt more real than many of the high-profile jobs I'd done before.

Later, someone said to me, "I really needed to hear that." Just a small comment. But it stayed with me. It reminded me that what I was doing mattered even if it looked different now.

Freedom, I've learned, isn't about doing anything you want. It's about choosing the things that mean something to you and letting go of what doesn't.

Soft retirement isn't about settling. It's about deciding. Not *stepping away from* life, but *stepping into* a better version of it.

If you're standing at the edge, wondering what's next, I want you to know you're not done. You're just getting started.

Sometimes, people ask me, "But don't you miss the structure?" And the honest answer is: not really. What I missed at first was a sense of purpose. But once I realised purpose didn't have to come from a job title, I stopped trying to replicate the past and started designing something new.

Structure is still there. I've just built it differently. Some days are for deep work, others for connection. Some for wandering, wondering, and letting things emerge. The rhythm of life in soft retirement is quieter, but more honest.

Value also changes shape. In the workplace, your value is often measured in outputs, targets, or how well you fit into a system. In soft retirement, it's measured in presence. In what you share. In how you listen. In the things you do that make someone else's path a little easier.

There's a quiet joy in mentoring someone who's just starting out. Or supporting a community project. Or helping a friend navigate something you've been through yourself. You stop chasing recognition and start finding meaning in the simple, everyday moments.

Legacy becomes less about big achievements and more about how you leave people feeling. Did you offer encouragement? Did you help someone believe in themselves again? Did you create something that helped someone else move forward?

If you've been in full-time work for decades, you've probably achieved more than you realise. But soft retirement offers you the chance to use that experience in new ways. It lets you stretch into roles that don't exist on a company org chart: the encourager, the guide, the quiet hand at someone's back.

I've learned that influence doesn't fade with age. It just moves behind the scenes.

It becomes deeper, more personal, and often more lasting.

So, if you're approaching this phase of life and feeling nervous, that's completely normal. There's no rulebook. No one-size-fits-all plan. But you're not doing it wrong. You're just writing your own version of what comes next.

And if you're unsure where to start, let me offer a few simple steps.

First, make space. Clear a little time in your week where you're not reacting to anything. No emails, no appointments, no tasks. Just quiet time to think, reflect, and reconnect with what matters.

Second, talk to someone. Not just about what you did, but what excites you now. Sometimes hearing yourself say it out loud is the first step toward clarity.

Third, say yes to something small. A coffee meeting. A one-off event. A project with no pressure. It doesn't have to be perfect. It just has to be possible.

And finally, remember that you're not alone. There's a growing community of INDYs out here. People who are saying, in all sorts of ways, "I'm not done yet."

You've earned the right to shape this next chapter however you want. So don't wait for permission. Don't wait to be invited.

This is your invitation.

Soft retirement isn't a trend or a lifestyle hack. It's a powerful, personal response to a changing world. A decision to live more freely, more intentionally, and more fully than ever before.

And if you ask me, that's not the end of anything.

It's the beginning of something wonderful.

About Andrew Middleton

Andrew Middleton is the founder of INDY *(I'm Not Done Yet)*, a peer network and movement for people exploring life beyond traditional retirement. After leaving full-time work at 58, Andrew coined the term "soft retirement" to describe a new way of living, one that blends purpose, flexibility, and freedom.

Drawing on a diverse background in senior leadership, charity work, and creative consultancy, he now supports others navigating the space between work and retirement.

Whether hosting events, running his online community, or answering emails from a beach, Andrew champions the idea that this stage of life is not about slowing down, but shifting focus. He writes and speaks about ageism, transition, and how to stay relevant and energised in your 50s, 60s and beyond.

Through INDY, Andrew brings together people who still have ideas to share, projects to build, and more to say. Because, as he puts it, "We're not done yet."

info@imnotdoneyet.co.uk

www.imnotdoneyet.co.uk

www.linkedin.com/andrewcmiddleton/

A Smallholding In Dorset? Maybe Not!

Sandi Goddard

Dorset. One of the most beautiful counties in the west of England. A land of soft, rolling hills, beautiful wooded valleys and breathtaking coastlines. Many summers tramping and camping in Dorset informed our retirement dream - a smallholding close to one of the beautiful villages that nestle near the sea.

The reality is, a smallholding needs a great deal of commitment in time, fit bodies, energy and, probably, money. We can only just cope with a dog and a middling-sized garden.

Instead, our next adventure will be to sell our home and... well, anything we want really!

This probably sounds as if we haven't given much thought to retirement. Not true. We have approached the prospect in quite a considered way.

However, we could certainly have started our financial planning when we were newly married, but life gets in the way... or I was simply bad at financial management. My mother's frequent advice: plan early for retirement.

I have been fortunate, rather than diligent, in that respect!

When we think about retirement there are four fundamental pillars to consider: funds, body, mind, and social engagement.

Board Leader Or Entrepreneur?

As you progress and make choices in your career, there will be a number of paths to travel. Each will have its own retirement considerations.

If you are a senior executive, retirement will not represent a simple wind-down. You will find it is a transition from a high-stakes decision-making world to one that is more self-directed. After years of driving growth, managing complexity and teams, and shaping your department or organisation, this transition can be liberating but it can also be extremely disorienting.

You will need to develop a new and deeply personal form of leadership. One that doesn't necessarily come with team support! But today, we have so many apps at our fingertips that can provide digitally what we lose in terms of personnel.

Entrepreneurs face their own unique challenges. You may have to navigate irregular cash flows, reinvestment pressures, and a mindset that can complicate things ... what is 'enough' in terms of funds?

Then there is the psychological challenge of leaving a venture that you have built. How do you reinvent your purpose and identity, once so closely aligned to your business?

For both a senior executive and an entrepreneur, it's about psychological preparation for a fundamental life change; from actively building and running your business to stepping back. It requires careful consideration of identity, purpose, and daily structure.

The most successful entrepreneurial retirement involves a gradual transition rather than an abrupt stop. And remaining engaged as you relinquish control.

The upside is the skills and connections that you developed as leaders will make you invaluable as Non-Executive Directors, Trustees, advisors and angel investors.

Money!

I recently read a WHO statistic about the dramatic rise in global life expectation. With improvements in health care, nutrition, lifestyle, you can live well past your late 70s and 80s, and beyond to 100, or more, that means retirement can last 25 – 40 years, or more.

Ideally, you need to be preparing for retirement from your 20s or 30s (NB. My mum's advice above!)

In general terms, the aim is to have 10-12 times your annual salary put aside for your retirement.

How you do this is not my area of expertise, so it's important to take advice from a Wealth Coach or IFA.

Body… And Mind

Elite performers often pay the price of success in mental and physical health. Retirement is a chance to recalibrate. Investing in your well-being should not be seen as a luxury; it's an imperative for the next phase of your life.

This is so much more than an annual checkup. It's learning how to sustain energy, sleep, nutrition, and strength. And develop mental resilience.

You may find the need for therapy, coaching, or reflective practice to process an identity shift and circumvent potential "post-retirement void."

But life is unpredictable!

As I get older, I am grateful that I am still active and my mental, and physical health is excellent.

A very, close friend of a similar age, has recently been diagnosed with vascular dementia. She is still young, but life has dealt her a pretty grim blow.

Fortunately, she has had a wonderful marriage and travelled extensively; her long-term memory is excellent, so her conversations are full of amazing anecdotes. And she is still able to maintain her engagement with others; as well as meeting up with friends, she belongs to a lunch club, choir and a book club.

We should never take our physical and mental health for granted. These are our most valuable resources

Don't Wait Until Tomorrow

This is a conversation about retirement, and retirement means different things to different people. But your preparation starts now!

Two of my favourite people aim to retire in their 50s so they are already working on interests that can become full time projects in retirement. Such a brilliant idea – none of us knows what will happen in the future.

Have you got a passion, a hobby that could become a retirement income? Don't wait until tomorrow.

Don't Make Work Your Life

A business colleague of mine lived to work, his time was consumed by it.

Now I love my work, I feel privileged to advise some amazing business owners, but I also have family and friends I want to spend time with and a wide range of hobbies that absorb me.

When my colleague retired, he had nothing to fall back on. His health had failed and he spent a great deal of his time in front of the TV.

Don't Give Up Work Too Soon

Yes, you can retire at 50 but will you be mentally and emotionally prepared?

I have friends who have taken early retirement, sold their businesses, etc, eagerly anticipating the freedom that retirement would bring, only to find that they weren't ready.

They missed the cut and thrust of business, the negotiations, the people and conversations. No matter how many cruises, holidays and projects they enjoyed, there was no comparison to the buzz they experienced in business.

A long-term business friend did just that. He sold his business and was excited about the new freedom to travel and enjoy life. One year, and several cruises, later he was bored and unsettled. He launched a new business and enjoyed another decade of success, before finally stepping down. At 80, he was finally ready for retirement.

A New Chapter – A New Adventure

Retirement is a time to reinvent, reconnect, and rediscover. It holds the potential for profound personal growth, purposeful contribution, and lasting joy.

Whatever age you decide to retire, whether you are in your 40s, 50s, or beyond, think of it as a transition to a new adventure, phase, project – another Start Up opportunity!

This is your time to try something new, to experiment.

Write a plan. Have a purpose. You could even develop a mission statement!

Your strategy for retirement could be developed on a White Board; picture all those dreams and hopes and bring them to life in retirement. Have you always wanted to do a road trip? Spend six months on a canal boat? Act? Sing? Play a musical instrument? Volunteer for an archaeological dig? Work with young people/animals? Why not? This is your time, now.

Lifestyle and Purpose

Find fulfilling and interesting projects.

The most successful retirees balance financial security with personal fulfilment. This may mean redefining business success into broader, life satisfaction, metrics such as those activities, relationships, and contributions that will provide meaning during retirement.

Philanthropy offers many entrepreneurs a pathway to continued impact and purpose. Establishing charitable foundations, supporting educational initiatives, or mentoring young entrepreneurs can provide the sense of building and contributing to something worthwhile.

Geographic considerations matter too. Some entrepreneurs prefer to remain in business-friendly locations where they remain connected to networks and investment opportunities, while others choose areas with lower costs of living, better climates, or enhanced lifestyle amenities.

And you may need additional funds for these lifestyles, so what hacks and ventures can you set up now that will provide you with passive incomes in retirement?

Friends And Family

Leadership and high-profile careers inevitably impact our personal lives, particularly in terms of time and attention that we give to our family and friends. Retirement can be an opportunity to re-connect, to engage meaningfully with those we love.

This is where GenZ may have a secret weapon. As you progress through your career, hang on to those values that are most important to you, they will benefit you later in life.

I love the way some cultures value family, live in compounds where they can care for cross-generations. We often walk past what we have decided is a 'family compound' near our home in Surrey. It is a large garden with three different sized houses – we imagine that the largest is the family home, the smallest for the grandparents, and the mid-sized is for the young marrieds with their infants.

Of course, this is not an option for most of us, but I have experienced the emotional and physical strain of living many hours from my parents, in their later life.

Friends of mine have had to work overseas or in the north of the UK, while their elderly parents lived in London or the West Country. They agonised over parental ill-health, felt guilty about not being closer, being able to support them physically and emotionally.

This is a debilitating, mentally and physically draining and expensive situation for our families.

My advice: move closer to family and friends in retirement.

Where would you rather be at end of life – being cared for and resident with strangers? Or able to visit and be visited by friends and family?

I firmly believe that the quality of life, our mental and physical health, is vastly improved by engagement with those we know, like and care about.

Think About Your Legacy

As your career progresses, your legacy will be your success in education, business, awards, recognition, wealth.

In retirement, it will be about impact. What do you want to be remembered for? What values are you passing on to the next generation? What knowledge have you accumulated over years of corporate or entrepreneurial life?

Retirement can provide the chance to shape that legacy, through your contribution to your next generation. Through mentorship, sponsorships, endowments and even a memoir that encapsulates your life and that of previous generations, an insight into how to build a great business, or a family history that will inform and inspire future generations.

You may decide to codify business lessons for the next generation. Or perhaps help your children develop financial maturity and ethical stewardship. Whatever form it takes, legacy is your last strategic project, and one that will transcend time and endure through the people you have touched.

I was introduced to Rotary some decades ago and became aware of the many opportunities there are to contribute to the communities that matter to me.

One business friend launched a charity to support primary and secondary education in Kenya, focusing mainly on girls. This is now an all-consuming endeavour that occupies him in retirement – as these young people gain awards, honours, degrees and jobs, they have become his enduring legacy.

Closer to home, I have many friends who work with local charities or national organisations, such as the Prince's Trust. So many organisations need expert knowledge and support – you will be spoiled for choice.

Finally

Whether you are a corporate executive, an entrepreneur or a business founder, the art of your retirement will be in designing your new life with as much clarity and intention as you once designed business strategies. This will be your most involved piece of work: crafting a life of meaning, impact, and enjoyment.

You will be redefining your relevance: your leadership becomes your legacy, your ambition evolves into contribution, and, most importantly, your personal freedom becomes your most valuable asset.

Like many of my entrepreneurial and corporate clients, you will have a pretty good idea about what you want from retirement. So, this is simply a series of anecdotes that might help you to crystallise and structure that final, successful, exciting phase of life.

About Sandi Goddard FioL

A Corporate Consultant and Executive Coach with over 35 years of entrepreneurial success, Sandi empowers business leaders with strategic insights, enabling them to build futures that resonate with their ideals and ethos.

Sandi's extensive experience in marketing and branding, including launching and managing successful creative advertising and marketing agencies, enables her to refine and define corporate narratives that align with overarching business goals.

Working with FTSE-listed organisations, and ONBs across diverse sectors, has informed her current role: preparing and enabling business leaders and boards to achieve demonstrably significant growth and profitable, £multi-million, returns and exit.

Sandi has contributed to five previous books authored by Andrew Priestley. She is a member of the Association of Coaching, Member European Mentoring & Coaching Council, a Fellow of the Chartered Management Institute and a Fellow of the Institute of Leadership & Management with Level Seven Accreditation

sandi@goddard-delaney.com

linkedin.com/in/sandigoddard/

facebook.com/sandi.goddard.5/

From Fear to Freedom

Ashley Edwards

Let's Be Honest - Retirement Is Scary

Just putting the words "plan" and "retirement" in the same sentence is enough to send some people running. The shutters come down. Minds switch off. The usual response is, "I've got plenty of time to think about that." I'm 53 - it's not far away now - and I'll be honest, I'm still scared. What will I do all day?

Retiring in our fifties we could actually be in retirement for 40 years which is as much time as some people spend working during their life. How scary is that!

People often say they can't wait to retire, but do they really mean it? Have they thought about their health? Their money? What if they're on their own? I actually am. I'm a silver splitter (not so silver however!) - which, in case you're not familiar, is someone who's divorced or separated later in life - and let me tell you, that fear hits differently when you realise you're navigating retirement on your own.

Why We Avoid Thinking About It

When we're young, retirement feels like some far-off concept. When I talk about retirement to my daughters, who are both in their twenties, they look at me like I've lost the plot. Then we hit our forties and fifties, and we still think it's miles away. Before we know it, we're on the doorstep of our sixties and wondering how we got here.

I've spent my whole life in financial services, mortgages mainly. I've had people in my ear about pensions, mortgages, savings - all of it. But my friends? My family? Not so much. And that's where I see the fear, the confusion, the "I'll deal with it later" attitude. But later comes faster than we expect.

Let's face it: retirement is a huge life change. And if we don't start preparing for it, emotionally and financially, it can hit us like a freight train.

Facing The Fear Of "Doing Nothing"

I'm not someone who sits still easily. I move from one thing to the next. I like to be busy. So the idea of waking up one day with no schedule, no goals, no routine - it freaks me out. I don't think I'm alone in that.

We spend our lives working, raising families, juggling responsibilities. Retirement, in contrast, is sold to us as this endless holiday - but is that really what it is? Is that what we actually want?

That's why I believe the earlier we face our fears about retirement, the more control we have over shaping it into something that works for us.

Not someone else's dream - our own.

The Three Types of Financial Mindsets

When it comes to finances in retirement, I see three types of people:

1. **The Legacy Givers** – These are the people who want to leave everything to their kids or family. Inheritance is the priority.
2. **The Life Enjoyers** – These ones want to spend what they've saved, treat themselves, and enjoy retirement to the fullest.
3. **The Balancers** – A bit of both. Enjoy now, leave some later.

I experienced the challenge of this in my last relationship where we simply could not agree on what retirement should look like. I wanted holidays, a house by the coast, a part-time job in a florist and endless cruises. I've raised my children to be independent and relying on me is not a position I want them to be in.

He wanted to save every penny he had to leave to his son and play golf in the countryside with the occasional trip – what we both wanted was not wrong, it was just different. But whichever group you fall into, combining finances with planning and retirement makes for a pretty intimidating trio. And yet - avoiding these conversations doesn't make them disappear. It only makes them harder later.

Facing the Truth of Retirement: It Might Not Be Ideal… But It Can Still Be Better

Let's be real for a moment. An idyllic retirement might not be possible- at least not the kind you see in the glossy marketing or even the one we imagine before we fall asleep at night.

You might not have much to play with.

You might be on your own.

You might be struggling with debt.

You might still have a mortgage- possibly an interest-only one- and be lying awake at night wondering what happens when that term ends (you may have heard of this as the term 'mortgage prisoner').

You might have health problems creeping in, and they're harder to ignore now.

You might desperately want to help your children or grandchildren, but feel like you're barely keeping yourself afloat.

You might be approaching retirement with nothing but a basic state pension and a mounting sense of dread.

This is reality for a lot of people. You are not alone.

The Hidden Trap Of Self-Employment

And here's something we don't talk about enough: if you're self-employed, you might be one of the biggest "head buriers" of them all.

Why? Because when you're employed, the system does some of the heavy lifting for you. Your employer automatically deducts pension contributions. You probably don't even think about it. It's like a background process- you get your payslip, the money goes in, job done.

But when you're self-employed, you are the system. I've worked directly with self-employed individuals for the last 10 years and there's no one taking money off you and tucking it away for your future. There's no HR team, no pension auto-enrolment, no reminders. Everything is on you. And that is terrifying for a lot of people.

The result? Many self-employed people put it off. For a month. Then a year. Then five. And before you know it, you're ten years in, with nothing set aside for retirement, and the fear becomes paralyzing. You tell yourself, "Next year." But next year never comes.

Let me be clear- if you're self-employed, you need to plan more than anyone else. You need to protect yourself, because no one else is going to do it for you.

But the good news is: you're also in control. You can make decisions. You can build flexibility. And you can take smart steps now to shape your future.

The key is to start. To face the fear instead of letting it dictate your future. Just like you show up for your business every day- you need to show up for your future too.

You're Not Alone - And You Don't Have To Be

So who do you talk to? Anyone! Literally - let's get that conversation flowing and out there. Your friends, your family, your neighbour, your bin man - who cares? You don't need to share your private financial details but ideas breed confidence and there is safety in numbers, right?

What about the professionals? There's a misconception that financial services people are all about numbers and jargon. But at their core, good advisers are people-people. They want to help. They want to listen. They're not there to push you into some big, scary decision on day one. I know this because I am one.

I say this with pride - because this is the industry I've been part of for decades. And I see the difference it makes every day. Helping people take the first step, clear their heads, and begin to imagine their finances, their home and their future - including a retirement that actually feels possible - it's why I wake up excited to do what I do. Honestly I do.

Don't be afraid of the word "advisor." Don't be afraid to ask questions. Your plan is yours alone - there is no "one-size-fits-all" and you can't pick a retirement off the shelf. Retirement planning is about your journey. Your fears. Your dreams. Your reality.

And sometimes, planning doesn't just involve financial advisers - it involves mortgage advisers, too. Sounds odd, right? Why talk mortgages when the goal is to pay it off before retirement?

Because some people won't manage that. And others might be sitting on a home that could help fund their retirement. "Later life lending" is growing fast. It's about leveraging your assets - wisely - to create the retirement you want. Not everyone will need it. But everyone should understand it.

Advice won't magically solve everything. It won't turn back time. But it will give you clarity. It will give you options. And with options comes a sense of control. Peace of mind. A plan you can actually work toward in your way - even if it's not perfect.

You might find you've got assets that can work harder for you. That your home can unlock freedom instead of just being a worry. That there are products and strategies and professionals out there who can help you live better, not just get by.

Trust me, I plan to use mine...

Have You Even Thought About What Retirement Looks Like?

Here's the question I want you to sit with: what does your retirement actually look like?

Are you going on cruises? Buying a house in Spain? Helping your kids onto the property ladder? Moving to the coast and walking your dogs on the beach every morning?

Have you written it down? Created a vision board? Can you picture yourself living it?

This isn't fantasy. It's your future. And once you've dared to imagine it, you can start to build a plan to make it happen.

Start Talking, Start Planning

I can be like a broken record, so here it is again: take advice.

Talk to someone. Talk to lots of people. You don't have to act on everything straight away - just start the conversation. Ask the questions. Think out loud. Be curious.

Define "regular" however it works for you - once a year, once every five years, every six months. But make it regular. That's how you stay on track. That's how you keep fear from taking over.

I talk to my financial adviser every February and have been doing this for the last 8 years. Has the fear gone? Not at all, especially as with every moment I am getting closer to 'that time' but what has happened is a sense of calm and a sense of reality – I know what I am playing with, I know what I need to do to try and get the life I want and I know what my retirement will look like even if I don't get everything I want. I just know more. It's comforting.

Replace Fear With Confidence

For me, retiring well isn't about perfection - it's about replacing fear with confidence. It's about having a plan. About knowing what you can achieve and living within that truth. Not your boss's truth. Not your friend's. Yours.

Let's be honest: life doesn't always go to plan. Relationships change. Careers shift. Unexpected things happen. But the sooner you give yourself permission to dream, to explore, to ask questions - the better your retirement will feel.

You deserve a retirement that isn't just about survival. It's about joy. Freedom. Possibility. But that won't happen by accident.

So let's end this chapter with a small, bold step: start talking.

And above all — doing something.

Because the worst thing you can do is nothing.

About Ashley Edwards

Ashley is a Senior Manager at a large UK mortgage business. She's been in financial services since the age of 16 - straight from school into banking, followed by 27 years in estate agency, and now over a decade in self-employed mortgage advice. It's been a fascinating ride, because for her, this world isn't about numbers -it's about people. She's seen lives up close: dreams, challenges, decisions, and surprises. As she often says - next to doctors, mortgage professionals probably know more about people than anyone!

Ashley lives a calm, simple life (her happy place), with two grown-up daughters and two very crazy French bulldogs. No grandchildren yet... but she's hopeful. Over the years, she's learned that as life goes on, your circle gets smaller and stronger - and she's all for that. A people person through and through, Ashley believes relationships - whether with clients or close friends - are everything.

That's why, after all these years, she still loves what she does.

ashleyer71@gmail.com

www.linkedin.com/in/ashley-edwards12

Retirement Is Not A Bed of Roses For A Serial Entrepreneur

Carl Adamson

"Fred's just retired. He won't last long!"

The words of my Grandmother to my Grandfather, about the man who lived next door. Fred had worked all of his life in "The Print", a common term for anyone who worked in the newspaper industry at the time, particularly those who worked in printing them. He drove to work in London everyday in his white Austin 1100. Early start and early finish. He was home by 2:30pm every afternoon.

Fred had just bought a new car for his retirement. A shiny new Austin 1100, this time in Harvest Gold, a mustard colour. It was Fred's pride and joy and he washed it every Sunday morning with a bucket of water and a sponge. He would then dry the car carefully with a quality chamois leather before applying copious amounts of wax and buffing it to a mirror shine. When he was finished, I could see my face in the chrome hub caps and shiny bodywork.

"Why?", my Grandfather said to my Grandmother.

"Because men like him fade away as soon as they retire",

she said. "He's only interested in cleaning his car. He never walks anywhere", she continued.

Sure enough, within a couple of years, Fred sadly passed away. He was only 67, a mere two years into his retirement.

That resonated with me deeply, even though I was only seven. From that moment on I associated retirement with end of life!

By contrast, my Grandmother deliberately kept my Grandfather active. They didn't have a car. They would walk to the shops together, arm in arm, six days a week

My Grandfather did a lot of reading. He would scour the newspapers from front to back, read books from cover to cover, and watched a lot of television documentaries. His brain was highly active. He spent a lot of time in the garden growing runner beans and tending his beloved roses. I would always stop and bury my nose in those roses and inhale their enchanting aroma, a habit that I never grew out of. For some reason it's rare to find fragrant roses today.

A few years earlier, when I was four years old and hadn't started school yet, I was sniffing the roses in my Grandfather's garden. He asked me, "What do you want to be when you grow up?". I didn't need to think about the answer, I already knew.

"I want to be a farmer with my own farm and a big red Massey Ferguson tractor," I replied.

Our garden backed onto a sports field where they cut the grass with a small red Massey Ferguson TE20 tractor. I would peer through a gap in the hedge for hours as it went up and down the field, filling the air with the fumes of Tractor Vaporising Oil (TVO), sweetened with the smell of freshly cut grass, yearning for my dream to come true.

But deep down, my dream wasn't about owning a tractor. It was more than that. It was about being my own boss. It was about being an entrepreneur.

Indeed, I grew up to be that entrepreneur. I owned the farm and a bright red Massey Ferguson tractor, much bigger than the one of my childhood dreams. But I wasn't a farmer, I was running my own business, an IT Consultancy. I remember having important business calls from the cab of my tractor, whilst mowing acres of grass with a nine-foot topper. Clients would joke and say that it sounded like I was inside a washing machine. "No, it's a tractor!", I always replied. A great conversation starter.

Yes, I fulfilled my childhood dreams and so much more. I have experienced many business adventures on my entrepreneurial journey. I do mean adventures, because that's exactly what they were and still are.

Retirement is a word that has long lost its appeal to me. No. It never appealed to me at all. While it may represent a golden era of relaxation, leisure, and long holidays for many, for me, it signifies something entirely different. Stagnation, irrelevance, and a dangerous slide into boredom. As a serial entrepreneur, I thrive at the sharp end, creating, solving, building, pivoting, and hustling. To even entertain the notion of retirement is simply terrifying. It's not just a lifestyle shift; it's a shift in identity, purpose, and vitality. It's a shift I have no intention of making.

In fact, the mere thought of retirement conjures an image of a man slowly spiraling into a pit of boredom, his sense of purpose eroding by the day. His identity and all that he stood for being chipped away until it's unrecognizable, until he is unrecognizable.

Dramatic? Perhaps. But it's an honest glimpse into how I view this end-phase of life that others so eagerly anticipate. For me, work isn't a burden to be escaped.

Rather, it's the source of my joy, curiosity, learning, fulfilment and contribution to the world.

My work truly is my *Ikigai*.

Work Is Not A Job, It's My Identity

Entrepreneurship isn't a phase in my life. It is my life. It's not something I've done to eventually stop doing. It's what I was born to do. It's how I explore the world, test my limits, and measure my impact. For me, it is the gym of life. I am hardwired to build businesses, to tackle new challenges, to problem-solve in high-stakes environments. That relentless curiosity and hunger for progress doesn't turn off at age 65, or 70, or even 90. If anything, it only deepens with age.

I've started and scaled companies, failed and succeeded, and then started all over again from nothing. There's a thrill in the chase, the uncertainty, the competition, the innovation. It keeps me sharp. It keeps me honest. It keeps me alive. Retirement would be like silencing a musician and telling them never to pick up an instrument again. It would be like blindfolding an artist and asking them to dispose of their brushes and take up fishing instead. That's not a reward. It's a slow death. In Fred's case it was a quick one.

For entrepreneurs like me, work is not separate from life; it is deeply intertwined with my sense of meaning. If I walked away from it, I wouldn't be walking toward fulfilment. I'd be walking into a void where intolerable boredom is the dish of the day, every day.

The Myth Of The Retirement Dream

Society sells us the dream of retirement as the ultimate goal: work hard, save up, and then finally live your life once you stop working. But this equation is flawed, at least for people like me. I am living my life right now. My work isn't something I endure in hopes of a future payoff. It is the payoff.

The irony is that many people discover too late that retirement is not all it's cracked up to be. The freedom they were chasing on the outside, often turns into captivity when they arrive on the inside. There's only so much golf you can play, so many beach resorts you can visit, so many Netflix shows you can binge before you start to feel irrelevant, unchallenged, and disengaged. The days stretch longer, not because they're peaceful, because they're empty.

Don't get me wrong, I value downtime, family time, social time, me time. They are all the life-changing impacts that most of us seek. The impacts that require a certain level of freedom to fully enjoy. The promise of that freedom, which retirement dangles like a carrot in front of us, for all of our working lives, is an empty one for entrepreneurs.

A promise that may sound attractive to someone who is an employee. The reward for a lifetime of faithful service to your employer. Parole for good behaviour at the end of a life sentence.

For an entrepreneur, retirement is a life sentence. An end of life sentence.

Mental And Physical Vitality Are Tied To Purpose

When the mind has no challenges to work through, it atrophies. When the body isn't in motion, it weakens. And when the soul has no mission, it starts to fade.

For me, staying active in business isn't about ego or addiction to work, it's about survival. It's about thriving well into the later stages of life, not limping toward the end. I want to wake up every morning with problems to solve, people to lead, innovations to chase, and value to create. That's how I stay sharp, energized, and alive.

Retirement, in the conventional sense, threatens all of that. It encourages disengagement when I want deeper engagement. It says, "You've done enough," when that doesn't even come close to my definition of done.

The Beauty Of Indefinite Work

I don't see my work life having an end date. And why should it? As long as I'm healthy, focused, and making a difference, why step away? The beauty of today's entrepreneurial world is that it doesn't require physical labour in the traditional sense. I can work remotely, build teams, consult, invest, mentor, and start new ventures well into old age. Many of the world's most respected entrepreneurs, are not slowing down, they're accelerating.

I see myself doing the same. Whether I'm launching new companies, mentoring founders, writing, speaking, or investing in ideas I believe in, I will keep going. There is no off-ramp, just new roads to explore. I've chosen indefinite work, not out of financial necessity, but because that's where I feel most alive and useful.

I don't envy those counting down the days to retirement. Because the real joy is not in escaping work. It's in finding work that excites you so much you never want to leave it.

A New Model For Living And Aging

"Good Morning, Carl. 1347!".

Those were the words of a senior team member in my client's business in London. He gave the same greeting every day. Only the number changed. It was counting down the days until he could retire. He loathed his job but had to serve the rest of his time before he was free.

We need a new model for aging, one that doesn't automatically include retirement as a mandatory milestone or a longed-for release date. For generations, people worked in jobs they didn't love, clocked in and out, saved diligently, and waited for the day they could stop. For them, retirement made sense. It was relief. But for people doing work they love, work that aligns with their talents and passions, stopping doesn't feel like relief, it feels like exile.

I reject the outdated idea that aging must mean disengagement. I'm not interested in slowing down for the sake of it. I'm interested in deepening my contribution, expanding my impact, and continuing to learn and grow. I've seen too many men retire and lose their edge, their purpose, and eventually, their lives, not because they were old, but because they stopped doing what made them feel alive.

If we want to thrive into our 70s, 80s, and beyond, we need to rethink the trajectory of our lives. It's not about peaking early and fading away. It's about staying in the game, finding new challenges, and continuing to write new chapters.

Retiring Thoughts: Choice Or Requirement

In the end, retirement is not a requirement. It's a choice and I choose not to retire.

I choose growth over stagnation. Purpose over passivity. Engagement over escape.

I will continue to work, not because I have to, but because I get to. Because the joy of waking up every morning with something meaningful to do is one of the greatest privileges of life. Because I know that as long as I'm contributing, I'm alive in the truest sense of the word.

So while others dream of beach chairs and slow mornings, I'll be dreaming up the next big idea, mentoring a startup, investing in innovation, or building something new from scratch.

Not retiring isn't a failure to move on, it's a decision to keep moving forward. And that's exactly how I want to live.

There are more like me. My clients are entrepreneurs too. But some of them are not what you might expect. They are octogenarians. Retirement does not sit well with them. Because retirement is not an age, even for those in their ninth decade of life. Retirement is a state of mind. When society expects them to be slowing down, they still yearn the thrill of the chase, their insatiable desire for learning drives them forward.

Society conditions us to believe that retirement is the ultimate destination. Play by the rules, follow the career map, climb the ladder, keep your nose clean, and if you live long enough, arrive at the magic destination. It's the socially accepted game of life.

But for true entrepreneurs, there is no magic destination. The real magic is in the journey.

About Carl Adamson

Carl Adamson is an experienced Business and Marketing Coach who helps business owners, amplify their personal brand and grow their businesses to win freedom to thrive. Having started his career in hospitality management, moving into retail sales management, before pivoting into a successful career as an IT Consultant and business owner, entrepreneurship is the driving force behind everything he does.

Using a 100% Agile approach, Carl led his team to win two coveted UK IT Industry awards for the Marine Data Exchange. It is now responsible for collecting and managing survey data throughout the lifetime of fixed and floating offshore wind projects around the British coastline.

As a Business and Marketing Coach, Carl leads with empathy, helping his clients to grow their businesses by adopting his P2P (People to People) mindset and leveraging persuasive Behavioural Science techniques to get more prospects to say YES and become fee-paying clients.

LinkedIn: *https://www.linkedin.com/in/carladamson11/*

https://carladamson.com/

https://deliverywithagility.com/

https://agilistix.com/

YouTube: *https://www.youtube.com/@DeliveryWithAgility*

Let Your Heart Sing

Kath Reade

During my retirement, I was board Chair of a number of NHS healthcare organisations, and I was asked to make a comparative study of health board governance between the UK and New Zealand and present a paper to an international conference at Auckland University.

On my first visit to a hospital in New Zealand I was delighted to meet Maori health system colleagues. I was intrigued to hear them introduce themselves in a traditional way linked to the land, by describing which mountain and river they were from. I followed suit, announcing 'I am Kath Reade from Pendle Hill by the river Ribble.'

It felt good. They then produced a guitar and sang a Maori song of welcome. Entering fully into the spirit of things, I asked to borrow their guitar. To their surprise I sang a self-penned song called *'Friendship'* which seemed to go down well. My visits went very successfully, with them opening to me fully and introducing me to some very moving scenes at a mental health community care facility. I thought of Aristotle opining that to be a good leader one must also know how to follow.

n my return to England my PA brought me a message from the Maori health workers which enclosed an album of Maori songs, and the words, 'We had previously thought English people were up their own a---s until we met you Kath. Thank you for listening to us.'

Retirement can certainly be exciting, and I have learned that leadership skills do not die in retirement, they are transferrable, and you can continue to be potent and relevant. Indeed, if these skills are in your makeup or an acquired skillset, you can flow in retirement to new and creative ways of allowing your leadership qualities to be expressed. You may find fulfilment for yourself or in service to others, or both. Above all, I hope you may agree, there must be meaning, and your heart must be in what you do to find the illusive quality of happiness in later years.

One of the benefits of a wiser older head may be that we are less likely to rush into ideas where angels fear to tread, and less likely to become entangled in activities we later come to sorely regret. This is not at all guaranteed however, as it is our little secret (don't tell the grandchildren) that we can be impulsive and heedless in later life when we do not listen to our infallible inner voice imploring us not to do whatever we are considering, and not to enter business relations with that person. You know the sort of thing.

I am a fan of mindfulness meditation. I suspect I am not the first to delve into the origin of the word *'retire'* and find it is traceable to the mid sixteenth century. A French word *'retirer'* is translated on Google as *withdrawing to a place of seclusion.*

It seems times have changed in the twenty-first century, as to retire often means to be encouraged to do the very opposite. To go out there and take risks. To explore, to travel, start businesses. To do everything possible to stave off ageing.

We are exhorted to see our trajectory as ever forward and upward.

However, in retirement we have the amazing gift of being able to step off the wheel however briefly, to come to a stop and to inhabit silence and stillness for a while. This may be sitting or walking. Our direction then can very profitably be in a downward or inner direction to explore the exciting depths of ourselves, and of existence, with all the proven benefits to our health, emotional resilience and sound decision making this undoubtedly delivers.

Moving relentlessly onward can mean never taking stock, never exploring stillness and silence, and experiencing its deep technicolour, kaleidoscopic, potential for inner travel, inner joy, deeper wisdom and insight.

The status quo is not actually static at all, and the ever-changing now of the present moment awaits your attention with life changing results. One of the revelations of becoming still and quiet is the truth that you are not your thoughts. Then you can rest in spacious awareness without being a prisoner of the crazy monkey mind as it is referred to in Buddhism. You can simply become the watcher of thoughts as they arise and pass.The usual method is to simply follow your in breath and your out breath, just as it is, and return to the breath whenever your mind wanders.

This is the germination of deep listening to who you really are. In this way it is possible to experience an inner peace you may not have known you were longing for. A quiet joy can follow on like ink spreading on blotting paper. I invite you to sit in silence and stillness for five minutes and that will be the beginning of cultivating a calm clarity of thought that will guide improved life decisions.

There can be a lot of static along the way, but it is worth persevering as disturbances are eventually resolved and will pass.

Being out in nature in quiet contemplation brings us to an authenticity, a sense of ourselves as part of the natural world. Living and breathing along with trees, our feet in touch with the energy of the earth, our faces turned towards the ever-changing skies and limitless cosmic energy. Then we understand the impermanence of everything, and how to fully appreciate the present moment.

After a while of these meditation practices, my whole attitude became more grateful, more peaceful, more able to be my true self. Stress gradually dissolved. Far from becoming passive and disengaged as I had feared, I found meditation to be the springboard to increased life force energy, and the foundation of spending my time doing the things I love. Meditation was energising!

This was important to me because I saw a danger in retirement of replicating the stresses and strains of my workplace career. I was very apprehensive that I would be looking into the abyss of not having anything to do. So I took on a myriad of roles and responsibilities in the early months and years of retirement, in all honesty, to compensate for a certain perceived loss of identity and status.

At first, I fell into the trap of frenetic activity. I trained as a Gong Master and Sound Healer. I became a qualified meditation teacher. I had a twenty-five-year Qi Gong practice (like Tai Chi) and began offering instruction. I was holding public classes and events weekly in all these modalities, in addition to writing a bestselling travel book and playing Singer-Songwriter gigs with my guitar. I was also mentoring Non-Executive Directors in board governance, and decision making.

And I was speaking at international conferences around the world on health and regeneration. I was still a member of several boards.

One of my last posts in the early years of retirement was Chair of Cumbria and Lancashire NHS Strategic Health Authority, which oversaw twenty-three healthcare trusts with an annual budget of £3,525 million. This was during the Blair government when waiting lists had to be reduced and A&E waiting times had to be a maximum of four hours or heads would roll. It was my job to ensure this was achieved for our communities. This kind of role can certainly bring retirement to life! For me it was a deeply held commitment to public service and my heart and head were fully devoted to my responsibilities. When this is so, many storms can be weathered and obstacles overcome.

When I decided that the next NHS reorganisation was one too many for me, I put my energies full time into my sound healing and meditation practice. While I received humbling testimonials and much moving positive feedback, I undoubtedly felt the challenge of losing the identity of my previous chair role. This puzzled me as I had always been rather diffident and self-effacing in my public sector leadership roles in the face of fawners and flatterers who I occasionally asked to stop it. Interestingly the fawners dropped me like a hot coal when I relinquished the role, and I went from 'hero to zero' overnight for the fair-weather friends.

My meditation practice helped enormously to distil what I wanted to do and to acknowledge the transience of everything once again. I was transformed by the wonderful practice of letting go.

In truth the greatest loss was of my PA. I have never quite got over that and now must plough through administrative tasks I once took for granted.

You see, I am much more fascinated with the beneficial effects on people's health and well being of specific sound frequencies. I am and have always been interested in what makes people the way they are, and my leadership style has always been encouraging, inclusive, and understanding how to motivate and empower people to realise their own talents.

From operating at the top of one of the largest most complex organisations in the world to working as a one-woman practice, I am still using my creative leadership skills. I am now in my element creating soundscapes with real benefit and beauty. Leading meditation, sound, and Qi Gong three-day retreats which are always full with a waiting list.

Along with competence and efficiency, and indeed hard-headedness when required, my work must always have, running through it, the essential life force of compassion and kindness. This is what makes the human connection and drives the life-affirming positive effects on those who partake. It also enriches trust and better decision-making.

I believe the greatest achievement in retirement is to engage in that which makes your heart sing, and even better if other hearts sing with you.

For me, none of this could be possible if I did not have at my core, the commitment to sit in silence and stillness for some time every day.

This is the bedrock, the saving grace.

About Kath Reade

A social worker and teacher, and highly respected public sector leader, Kath was latterly Chair of Cumbria & Lancashire NHS Health Authority, and was awarded Outstanding NHS Chair by the NHS Leadership Academy for her work to tackle health inequalities and her expertise in Governance.

Throughout her life Kath has always been a singer-songwriter and writer. Now in her 70s, Kath is also a trained sound healer, Qi Gong practitioner, and meditation teacher with a loyal following.

She is an international speaker and best selling author with many well reviewed albums of her songs.

'Kath Reade's voice has the silken quality of Bailey's Irish Cream' - Keely Hodgson of The Purple Room 21/9/24

Kath now runs sought after music, qi gong and meditation retreats in the beautiful Lake District and Yorkshire Dales.

Kath lives in Burnley, Lancashire, in England with her husband Paul who is a retired IT professional and a folk singer.

She has one son, Shaun, who is a musician and IT business owner.

www.kathreade.co.uk

Retirement A Loss Or A Gain? Your Choice

Jessica McGregor Johnson

Retirement can be a three-sided coin. For some it is looked forward to and even longed for and feels like freedom after decades of hard work. For others, even though they know it's coming it can feel daunting, and the closer it gets it can feel like a real loss of a very big part of who you are. And the third side of the coin are those who are "being retired". This has an even more complicated psychological impact because the timing does not feel in their choice and so not only might there be a loss of identity but there can also be a feeling of rejection.

The key to having a happy retirement in all of these cases is planning. Knowing what is coming and having thought about it, considered it,and planned for it. I recently had a client on a retreat and even though he had plenty of money for his retirement one of his biggest concerns was not having an income. Not that he needed an income, but the income gave him a validity, it was how he had measured his value to himself, his family, and the world.

This planning is different from the financial planning that will have started many years previous. This planning for retirement tends to take place in the last year of work.

Up until that point retirement has seemed like a great thing out there in the future, but when you get close to it the potential losses need to be addressed. In this planning you'll want to be looking at what gives meaning in your life, where you'll find a new feeling of purpose, creating a new identity that isn't based on your work, seeing where you can feel useful and contribute.

The Loss Of Identity

This can be a huge stumbling block for some people when they're retiring, particularly if they've had a successful and busy career. If you think about it, one of the first questions we're asked when we meet new people is what do you do? It's the opening gambit of getting to know somebody and one of the hardest questions for somebody who's newly retired, who hasn't grabbed it with both hands, to answer with a good feeling. "I'm a CEO," "I'm a teacher," "I'm an engineer," "I'm a doctor," "I'm a nurse," "I'm a CFO" - all these answers, and any others that you could give depending on where you have focused your career, have defined you for years.

They define you in relationship to yourself, how you feel about what you've done, what you've achieved and where you've decided to put your years of effort. But they also define you in the eyes of others. Whether that's good or bad, it is just what happens in our society. When we answer that question when we're still working it gives us a feeling of security, people can know who we are by what we do. Not that that is actually true, we are far more than our title and our job, but we have got so used to being identified by it that when we lose it on retirement it feels like a very big loss.

The workplace also gives us a context of who we are, we have different relationships with different people in the workplace and those relationships give us a sense of self. Remove that, and you remove a large part of your identity.

The Loss Of Purpose

This can be as simple as the loss of routine, we may have complained about the routine of work when we were in it, but suddenly not having it can make us feel a loss of sense of direction and meaning.

Not only that, in most roles we are part of a team or have working colleagues that depend on us, this gives us a sense of community and purpose, there's a reason that you do what you do.

Without the demands of your role, life can almost feel a bit aimless or meaningless, you start to question what am I supposed to do now? This is not a small question - we all need purpose in our lives. At this time in life it is a matter of shifting your focus and finding something that has a feeling of purpose that is not tied in with the purpose of your previous career.

The Loss Of Usefulness And Contribution

One of the biggest motivations in our working life, is the sense of feeling useful and being able to contribute to something larger than ourselves. As human beings it is part of our genetic makeup to want to be part of something. In some careers, that part of something is a huge belief in what you are doing in the company or what the company offers. Or maybe you own the company and feel it is contribution in many ways. Feeling that your role in this company is useful to society and contributes can bring a great feeling of personal satisfaction. Whether it be building a product, helping people, innovating new ideas, taking care of people in large companies. All these things have a feeling of usefulness and contribution.

I had a client who was retiring come on retreat, and one of his main things was he felt he wanted to leave a legacy of some kind. He always thought this would be through his work, but he came to realise that there were many different ways to leave a legacy. For him he saw his passion was actually his family, he could focus on his family and supporting his children and that in itself would be a powerful legacy to continue through the generations.

Working out that you still have something to offer, that you can still feel useful in new and different arenas is a key part of retiring happily, being forward focused as you move into this next era.

The Inner Impact

A lot of focus is around the financial side of retirement and not so much is focused on the psychological and inner impact retirement can have. Without planning, people can get into depression, particularly if the transition is not managed well. Not only that, if there is nothing planned that you could step into, loneliness can become quite a large issue. We often hear of people who retire and die quite quickly afterwards and although there might not be a direct correlation, as human beings we need interaction, purpose, an identity to feel healthy both mentally and physically.

"Being Retired"

This can be a very challenging situation, for most people it happens in their late 50s, they feel they have quite a few years left to offer their expertise, to contribute. Suddenly through no fault of their own - more often than not a merger or acquisition - they find their role is redundant. Even if these people have an idea of what their retirement will look like, the fact that it's been brought forward by five or maybe more years is it hard. Yes, they financially might be in a perfectly fine situation but that doesn't stop the psychological impact of suddenly no longer working.

I had a client come out on my *Retire Happily* retreat in just this situation. The first thing he said to me is "I have to find a new job". I said maybe not, let's just explore this for a couple of days. We came up with the phrase "what would it look and feel like to live a bloody wonderful life?" When I first asked this, he looked at me as I had two heads, but on discussion he realised that he could give himself permission to just enjoy the next bit of life. Yes, there was definitely some work to be done around identity, purpose, usefulness, but that first step of him giving himself permission to take this opportunity and go out and live a great life was like a door opening in front of him. Suddenly this vista of how he and his wife could enjoy the next years became possible.

The Four Stages Of Retirement

As Dr. Riley Moynes said in his TED talk there are four stages of retirement.

1. The first is the *vacation stage* where you stop, maybe even go for a long holiday, and just get used to having no demands.
2. The second stage is where you start to *feel the losses.*
3. The third stage is when you go into a panic mode and *feel you need another job* to fulfill your purpose in life.
4. And the fourth stage is *reinvent,* when you realise that there are different ways to address these losses and you move into the next era of life where you are creating a different meaning, a different identity and a different way to contribute.

Reinventing

I'm a great believer that with retirement planning you can skip stage 2 and 3 and go straight from *vacation* to *reinvention.* This *definitely* takes some work and some reframing of how you look at yourself, but in all the times I've been working with retirement retreats this is the focus that has made the difference.

So How Do You Do It?

Your Identity. Start with looking at how you identify yourself. Instead of just using your job as your identifier, write down all the different roles you play for different people in your life. Friend, Supporter, Spouse, Parent, Child, or Sibling. Those are just the more intimate identifiers of who we are. Then look at what you love; are you a sports person, do you love mentoring, maybe working with young people. Start to see that you are so much more than your old role. And reframe that role so for example" I was a teacher" becomes "I'm a lifelong educator and mentor." "I was a doctor" becomes "I'm a carer." Start to look at yourself through a different lens.

New Purpose. Look back through your life and look at where it has felt most purposeful. Not necessarily just during your career but in all of your life. Identify what pursuits you were doing at that time that made it feel so purposeful. Focus in on the details, so say for example one of your purposes in life has been to be a parent, don't leave it just there, focus in what is it about being a parent that feels so good. Flesh out the purpose and see where it leads you.

Feeling Useful, Contributing. Start to look for other ways that you can start to feel useful. This can be within your close circle of family or friends or, you might look outside that to your local community. I had a client who went back and started a local repair drop in within his village. Instead of things being chucked away he got together all the people who loved to tinker and mend things and every month they came together in the village hall and people brought things for repair. Not only did it make him feel useful and connected but he also felt he was contributing to the environment because not so much stuff got thrown out without a chance for a second life.

Stay Connected. it is really important that you maintain social ties to stop the feeling of being isolated. If you already have a wide circle of friends, even if some of them are still working, you have to have regular times when you meet up. One of the ways to make sure that you keep seeing your friends, particularly if they're busy, is that when you leave whatever meet up you've had with them you arrange the next date. This is also very good for you mentally so you have things in the diary to look forward to. If you haven't invested in friendships maybe now is the time, local community groups are great for making new connections and nowadays with the technology you have we can stay in contact with people who aren't even local. It is crucial that you stay connected with other people as it's a proven buffer against isolation and depression.

Allow Whatever You're Feeling

It is normal to feel a level of grief when you leave behind something that's been a huge part of your life for so many years. One of the things that grief counselors will tell you is to allow yourself time to grieve, but don't wallow in it. If you feel you're grieving a lot, give yourself some time every day to allow yourself to really feel the feelings. But once you've done that for that limited period, it's time to get up, get out and get into life.

Retirement is a big shift in life, it's one of the biggest changes we go through. There are many people who have not yet retired because they simply can't work out what it's going to look like. This is a shame because retirement, when you grab it with both hands and wring the joyful juice out of it, can be one of the greatest times in life. More time with your family particularly if you have grandchildren, more time to go and do the things you've never got around to, more time to stop and simply enjoy life.

All you need to do is plan it.

And remember you can also plan it together as a couple to make sure that both of you get equal billing!

About Jessica McGregor Johnson

Jessica is an international coach and retreat facilitator. Jessica's signature programmes are her individual and couple retreats - *Retire Happily* - ensure your retirement is meaningful fulfilling and fun and *Get Unstuck* - reset the course of your life. In her 22 years of working in this field she has seen how important planning is for retirement and so created a retreat specifically for it to make sure that retirement is the cherry on the top.

Living in southern Spain where she offers her retreats, she has been described as "way more than a coach, a wise voice that guides you to clarity to create the best scenario possible."

As well as Co-authoring *Retire Inspire 1*, and *Retire Inspire 2*, she has also written two books: *Remembering Perfection*, and *The Right T-Shirt* - write your own rules and live the life you want.

https://jessicamcgregorjohnson.com

https://www.linkedin.com/in/jessicamcgregorjohnson/

Between Two Generations

Karen Frith

I never want to retire, but I need work to leave room for moments my parents may not remember, and my children will never forget.

Right now, I'm in the middle of those two worlds. My dad is living with dementia. He still knows me, most days. Other days he asks if I've seen his brother, or if I've finished my homework. And then there's my daughter - on the edge of everything, needing lifts, food, time, and conversation I don't always feel able to give.

Around me, friends my age are leaving long careers. Some jump. Some are pushed. All of them are wondering what comes next.

They're tired. Decades of long days, late nights, and workplace politics have worn them down. So the idea of early retirement feels like a relief.

But in quieter moments, many admit they're not sure they're ready to stop. They don't want to do nothing. They just want to do it differently.

That's exactly where I was a few years ago.

Tired, but not done yet. I had built a successful career - senior roles, big clients, strong networks – and I was proud of what I'd achieved.

But I could feel something shifting. Dad was starting to slip. My kids were hitting mayor exam years. And I had this growing sense that if I kept working the same way, I'd miss everything important.

So I started asking a better question: what if I didn't retire - but I did redesign?

I didn't have the answers straight away- but over time, ten things stood out.

#1: Your Experience Still Matters

After three decades of work, it's easy to feel like your best contributions are behind you, like you've peaked. But that's not true.

The things we've learned over the years - how to lead through crisis, how to calm chaos, how to deliver what really matters- those are exactly what clients and organisations still need.

What's changed is how that value is delivered. I no longer believe value comes from being present every day from nine to five. It comes from solving the right problem, making the right thing happen and helping people move forward.

Years ago, I took on a short contract to help a retail client streamline their communications strategy. The work was outcome based. Clear deliverables. Clear timeline. No long meetings. No noise. Just clarity. I worked early mornings before school runs and blocked a few afternoons for deeper sessions. It fit around my life and delivered exactly what the client needed.

It was the first time I thought, maybe I don't need to walk away from everything I've built. Maybe I just need to deliver it on my own terms.

#2: Flexibility Isn't A Luxury… It's A Design Decision

When people talk about flexible working, they often think of it as a benefit or a bonus. For me, it became essential. Dementia doesn't respect calendars. Neither does parenting. I needed a structure that gave me space when the family needed me and clarity when clients did.

So I built three rules into every piece of work:

1. The work must be outcome anchored. If we can't define success in a few clear sentences, we don't start.
2. The work must be schedule neutral. I carve out specific times for live calls. The rest happens on my time, not theirs.
3. The work must respect my energy. If a task drains me, it gets automated, delegated, or timeboxed. If it energises me, it gets priority.

This isn't about being difficult, it's about being deliberate. Time is precious. My best work happens when I'm clear about how and when I can deliver it.

#3: Energy Is Currency, Spend It Wisely

Supporting a parent with dementia isn't something you can plan. Some days, Dad is calm. Other days he's confused and scared. I've had video calls rescheduled because he needed help getting dressed. I've paused reports mid-sentence to guide him back to his chair.

It's not dramatic. It's just real life.

And that emotional load doesn't clock off at five. So I learned to build recovery into the rhythm of my week. Ten minutes of quiet before a visit. A walk after the hospital. Friday mornings with no meetings and a blank notebook. These aren't indulgences. They're how I protect my capacity to think clearly and show up fully.

The truth is, if you want to do meaningful work at this stage in life, you have to be just as intentional about rest as you are about results.

#4: Let Systems Do The Talking

A while back, Dad had a bad fall. I was at the hospital for hours, barely touching my phone. But the client project still moved forward. Why? Because I'd already built systems that didn't rely on me being available every minute.

- Project dashboards updated in real time
- Weekly status emails sent automatically
- Pre-recorded explainer videos that clients could watch whenever they needed

These things don't make the work impersonal - they make it sustainable. Clients still feel looked after, they get the support they need and I get the space to manage whatever's happening at home.

#5: Price For Peace Of Mind

One of the reasons people fear leaving full-time work is money. I get that. It's a real consideration. But I've found that when you stop charging for hours and start charging for outcomes, you can create a business model that gives you both income and margin.

I build a contingency into every quote. Not because I expect disaster, but because life happens. University expenses, car repairs, unexpected respite care. That buffer gives me the freedom to say no when something doesn't feel right - or to step away briefly without everything falling apart.

#6: The Family Calendar Is A Business Tool

We run the family like I'd run a project team…

Colour-coded calendars.

Shared reminders.

Weekly check-ins.

It sounds rigid, but it's the opposite. Because everything is visible, it's easier to move pieces around without stress.

Blue is for medical appointments. Green is for client work. Yellow is for rest and recovery.

Everyone sees the whole picture. It removes guilt, stops clashes, and gives us all a sense of rhythm in a time of life that can feel chaotic.

#7: You Don't Need To Do This Alone

There's a myth that stepping away from traditional employment means stepping away from community - I've found the opposite.

The best thing I ever did was connect with others doing similar work. Consultants, creatives, coaches - all bringing decades of experience to the table and choosing flexibility over formality.

We share resources. We cover for each other. We ask honest questions when things feel heavy.

It's not just about support. It's about perspective. When you see other people building lives that balance care and contribution, it's easier to believe it's possible for you too.

#8: Crisis Comes... Be Ready

There's a simple framework I use when things get disrupted. I call it the Three Ps:

1. **Protect people.** Let the client know what's happening. Be honest and calm.
2. **Protect outcomes.** Review what's urgent, renegotiate where needed.
3. **Protect energy.** Drop anything that isn't mission-critical and restore later.

That's it. No drama. No over-explaining. Just grace and clarity. And every time I've had to use it, clients have responded with understanding, not judgement.

#9: This Is Still Legacy Work

It took me a while to realise I didn't need a job title to create impact. Every proposal I write, every workshop I run, every piece of clarity I help a client achieve - it all matters. It's all legacy work.

More than that, I know my children are watching. They see me doing work that supports others but doesn't come at the expense of being present. They see me holding space for their grandad. They see what it looks like to care and contribute at the same time.

This version of working is not about stepping down. It's about stepping in - more intentionally, more flexibly, and with more humanity than the corporate version ever allowed.

#10: You Can Lead Without A Title

One of the strange gifts of this season of our lives is realising that leadership doesn't depend on a job description. When I left my full-time role, I assumed I was walking away from leadership. No team. No org chart. No direct reports.

But leadership kept showing up. It looked different.

It showed up in the way I briefed a nervous client team through a major change with calm, clear language.

It showed up in the way I helped my kids navigate a complicated friendship issue without jumping to solve it.

It showed up in the way I advocated for Dad during a medication review, translating jargon and asking the questions others were too rushed to ask.

Leadership, I've learned, is less about authority and more about presence. Less about power and more about clarity. It's the steady voice. The person who notices. The one who brings the temperature down and shows people the next step.

That's a kind of leadership that doesn't retire. It just evolves. And it's needed everywhere.

So What Do We Call This?

I didn't have a name for what I was doing at first. I just knew I needed to earn money without burning out - and still be around for the people who needed me most.

That was the moment it clicked -I'd been doing what's now known as "Fractional Consulting

It describes exactly what I do. I bring years of knowledge and experience to clients in focused, scoped ways.

Not full-time, not forever just for now.

Projects are delivered with experience and care. It's not about being "less than." It's about being precisely enough.

Fractional work isn't a second-rate option. It's a high-impact way to keep using everything you've built while gaining the space to live the rest of your life on your terms.

If You're At The Crossroads...

You don't have to retire just because you're tired of how work used to be. And you don't have to keep going like nothing's changed. There is another way.

You can design a rhythm that holds your professional expertise and your personal reality with equal respect.

You can deliver high quality work without being on call 24/7. You can earn well, work with people you like, and still be there for ageing parents and growing kids.

You can build something that doesn't ask you to forget who you were… or ignore who you are now.

Final Words From The Ward

Dad's eyes close and his hand tightens gently around mine. I sit with him until the lights dim. My phone pings again - his time with a "thanks" from a client who's just watched the video summary I sent this morning.

It feels good. No chasing, no crisis, just progress.

This is the season I'm in. Holding space for my dad. Guiding my kids. Helping clients move forward.

I don't want to retire from that.

I just want to do it in a way that makes room for what matters.

I can… and so can you.

About Karen Frith

Karen Frith is a passionate champion of the freedom and flexibility that fractional consulting offers. As founder of Greenlight Partners and the Fractional Academy, she helps independent consultants thrive on their terms – matching top talent with forward-thinking organizations that value agility and impact.

Karen began her career in accounting but soon realized she wanted more autonomy and purpose. Transitioning into contracting, and later fractional consulting, she found a path that allowed her to build a business and life she loves.

Through her work, Karen not only opens doors for consultants but also creates a vibrant, supportive community - something often missing in solo careers. Her transatlantic perspective, spanning the UK and US, brings global insight to modern consulting.

With a straight-talking style and real-world wisdom, Karen empowers others to take control of their expertise and build businesses they're proud of. Whether through her work, webinars, or this book – Karen's mission is clear: your next chapter starts now.

Greenlight Partners: https://www.greenlight-partners.co.uk/WANDY
LinkedIn: https://www.linkedin.com/in/karenfrith/

Nesting for Old Age Wasn't for Me - Three Ideas for Early Retirement

Steven Shove

As I write these words, I am sailing my yacht in the Caribbean.

I am not an excessively rich man monetarily but am leading the richest of lives imaginable. I have followed good advice and achieved the outcomes I had dreamt of.

In *Retire Inspire 1*, I set out the idea of achieving a balanced portfolio for retirement. A balance between health, wealth, community, contribution, and growth. Indicators to help you both prepare for and thrive during retirement, satisfying both the physical and emotional needs of life.

I also suggested that retirement in the traditional sense need not be the only path to follow, and that a life that balances and blends the best of ones working life and that of a traditionally retired person might be more suitable for this modern age.

In this chapter of *Retire Inspire 2*, I introduce three additional ideas that I hope will act as catalysts that inspire you to transition towards this incredible stage of life.

hey may help you to answer three common

- *..u to retire?*
- *what will retirement look like?*
- *Is it the right thing for me?*

I will also share with you some of the barriers I faced and how I overcame them, plus how I plan to sustain things going forward.

Idea #1 - Enough Is As Good As A Feast

These seven short words quite literally transformed my life and freed me to live a life of adventure and exploration, to live on my own terms, confident that I could take certain risks to maximise life now and not wait until some point in the future when I could perhaps more comfortably do so. These few words would also allow me to retire early.

The reality is that we all need far less than we think we do.

"Achieving more with less" is a tenet of the *ReallyWild Method*® on which I built my businesses, but it rings true even today. By having fewer things and living more simply I have been able to retire at least a decade earlier than I might have done. I have been able to create a life that balances the retirement activities I pursue with the work I choose to do as well, not worrying unduly about the financial ramifications.

In the year leading up to my retirement (which I intend to keep as a state of semi-retirement) I sold or gave away most of my possessions, moved to a smaller home (in fact onto a boat), decided to keep the businesses small and manageable even in my absence, and cut my cloth to live richly in an affordable way.

Being with a woman who was already used to living minimally and spontaneously with a mutual sense of adventure, made it even easier.

As our friends were "nesting for old age" (a phrase I light-heartedly coined for their activities), doing up or extending their houses for example, even raising garden borders in preparation for when they might not be able to stoop so low, my partner and I decided to go back to our teens. We decided to learn to sail and explore the world with little to no experience.

I struggled with the notion that "sensibly" I should work for a few more years to get more money behind me, only to stumble across a sailing phrase that helped change my mind.

Go small, go now!

The phrase refers to buying a cheaper and more modest boat that will absolutely do the job but might not have all the bells and whistles on it. By doing so, a person is far more likely to put to sea and in fact see the world rather than dreaming of it whilst increasing the risk of never leaving shore.

We bought a modest yacht and set sail quickly.

Moreover, because of our boat's simplicity we have been able to sail most of the time, visiting remote islands and reefs, swimming with sea turtles and sharks and enjoying experiences most might only dream of. Friends with far more impressive vessels have generally spent substantially more of their time at the dockside as one state-of-the-art system after another has let them down.

Others are still waiting for the perfect yacht to come along.

Pursuing more than you need can not only delay your plans but add unnecessary complications, stress, anxiety and frustration.

In the moments when we sit on deck blanketed by the stars with the brilliance of the sunset still burning in our minds, my partner and I will often count our blessings and remember those who have not been able to pursue their dreams. Too many have either passed away too soon or become ill when they could have afforded to retire quite comfortably so many years earlier. This is the reason I decided to write this chapter.

Enough truly is as good as a feast!

Idea #2 - Coddiwomple!

"So, Steve, what are you going to do?"

We had fired the gun and embarked upon our retirement journey, quite literally without knowing where we would go, not knowing exactly how we would get there and what we would do once we arrived.

We had already downsized our lives, my partner had resigned from work, and we had set a date for when our new lives would start.

My unease at not knowing exactly how to answer the very understandable questions raised by our friends and family was palpable, until that is, I came across a word that described what we were doing perfectly.

As soon as we read its meaning, our concerns melted away and our resolve that we were doing the right thing multiplied.

"Coddiwomple" is the word, and it means to travel purposefully towards an unknown or vague destination, focusing on the journey or experience itself rather than the exact end point. It embraces a sense of uncertainty and the potential for unexpected discoveries along the way.

Not having an exact plan was no longer a reason for delay, rather a reason to head out anyway, somewhere or anywhere, provided it helped us achieve what it was we were sure we wanted to enjoy – a balanced portfolio of experiences that would enable us to thrive.

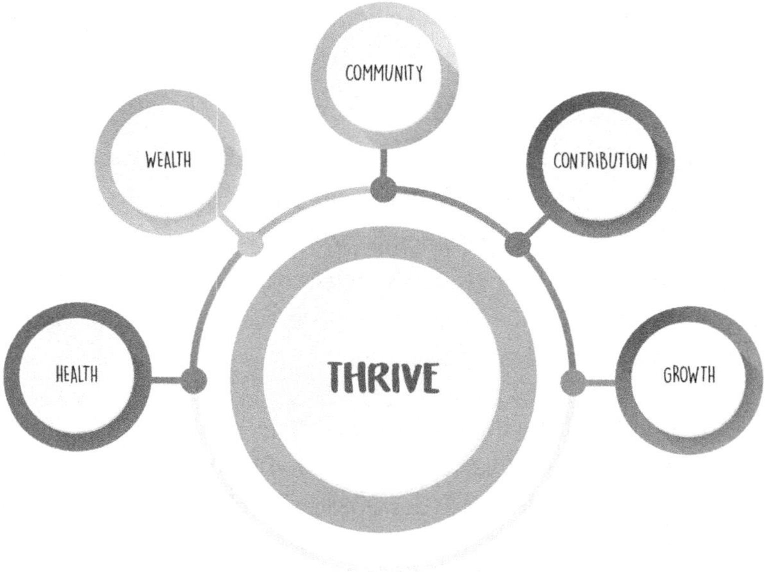

In my case, I broadly knew I wanted the following:

- **Health** – An activity filled life with great food
- **Wealth** – Having enough to enjoy life comfortably with back up for emergencies
- **Community** – A great social and family life meeting new and interesting people
- **Contribution** – Helping others or the world in a meaningful way
- **Growth** – Learning new skills, living a life of adventure and developing as a person

I had a few of these in place already.

We had worked on becoming healthier and were feeling the benefits of running, swimming and yoga and wanted to achieve more. We had downsized and cut our cloth to enable a degree of financial freedom and wanted this to continue. We had a wonderful community around us but looked forward to meeting new and more varied friendship groups with people from different backgrounds. We kept our small businesses so we could continue to support our customers but wanted to help other audiences in other ways too.

We were now about to step so far outside of our comfort zones that to grow could be the only possible outcome. Either that or we could face utter annihilation. Sailing would be involved which brought with it risks, especially for such inexperienced people. We didn't know how or where this would take us, but we knew it would be an adventure.

So it was against this backdrop that one night we found ourselves in front of a laptop, determined to book flights before bedtime to an undecided destination. Would it be Asia, the Americas, Antipodes, Caribbean or Europe?

We were intent on travelling purposefully towards an undetermined or vague destination ...and that made all the difference.

Our purpose and therefore destination was simply a desire to meet and enhance our five criteria of health, wealth, community, contribution and growth. And if we made a mistake, we had already told those people dearest to us that at least we would have tried and would return with our heads held high, to carry on where we left off until we developed another plan.

In the words of Theodore Roosevelt, *"Better to have tried and failed than to never have tried at all."*

Our fingers hovered over the *"Book Now"* button, and together we clicked on it. This set our course for the Caribbean.

A great many more things happened that ultimately determined where we would end up, on which boat we would sail, and how we would become competent to do so. Our lives had been enriched on every front.

Our health had improved dramatically with the physicality of living at sea and eating a different diet, our costs although initially high had become entirely manageable, we'd met people of different walks of life and backgrounds we hadn't imagined, contributed in a small way to a community of hurricane victims, developed new skills and learned more about ourselves, each other and our relationship than we might ever have thought possible.

We had fired, aimed very generally in a broad direction, and only then once fully committed, become anything like ready to succeed. "Ready, Aim, Fire!" had become "Fire, Aim, Ready!" and we had thrived.

It seems to me that many people never quite feel ready to retire for fear of not knowing what on earth they will do. Professionals who are used to following very specific plans in the workplace might naturally feel uncomfortable without a similarly well-defined plan for retirement.

If instead, they embrace the idea of the *"Coddiwomple"* and head off anyway, guided only by the five general principles I have set out above, they may find themselves at an as yet unknown destination that could surpass their wildest expectations.

Worst case, they will likely have enjoyed an amazing journey on the way.

3. Put Yourself At The Centre

The questions I had about my obligations to those I most cared about were of real concern to me when making the decision to retire and to begin so by travelling.

My father had pointed out to me that for years, in fact for most of my adult life, I had been putting the needs of others before my own, and that I had reached a point in my life when perhaps I should put my own needs first. He said that if I put myself at the centre then everything else would look after itself.

He was right.

My children, parents, close friends and colleagues have fared well in my absence and by my stepping back, I've been available to support them and stay in touch remotely and have done so full of energy and joy. I know that should any of them really need me in person or otherwise I will be there for them, prepared to change plans or redesign my life should the need arise. But for now, I have my window of opportunity and have taken it, and it has been a positive experience for all.

Summary

Enough is as good as a feast – You may be able to retire earlier than you think and can do so with far less stress and anxiety by keeping things modest. Go small, go now!

Coddiwomple! – You don't need a detailed plan, just some key principles by which to evaluate your choices. A balanced scorecard to live by will help achieve a rich and amazing life.

Put yourself at the centre – If you have a window to retire or do something incredible for yourself, take it! You can always change things later if you need to.

With respect to sustaining my own retirement, my plan is to adhere to the principles and ideas I have described. They have served me well and continue to do so.

About Steven Shove

An author, coach, adventurer, businessman and survival skills instructor, Steven is creator of the Really Wild Method® a powerful and proven methodology for success that uniquely equips and enables individuals and organisations to deliver superior performance and wellbeing with far greater consistency and predictability.

He is currently semi-retired, living a life between the Caribbean and Europe on his two yachts.

Steven is CEO and Founding Director of the Really Wild Group which offers personal development experiences, expeditions and retreats around the world, focusing predominantly on life changing experiences delivered within the UK and within the Arctic Circle.

Having applied his methods successfully to help people transition through many of life's key stages, he is now increasingly focused on supporting those planning to make the most of their retirement.

LinkedIn: Steven Shove

Facebook: Steven Shove and Really Wild Academy

www.reallywildacademy.com

www.reallywildbusiness.com

Whatsapp: +44 (0)7771 520515

Retiring Well... The Transition To The Next Chapter

Catherine Rolt

Treat this chapter as if you had decided to invest in being with an Integrated Health Practitioner who would support you in making this next transition the most invigorating and alive that you have had so far.

It is said in Traditional Integrated Medicine that by the time we have passed our 40 and 50's, we have had the opportunities to weave together both our sexuality and our spirituality. The two most powerful aspects of ourselves have become comfortable and have ignited our internal power batteries as we have matured.

Which means what, and how is it connected to the concept of retiring well !? Well....A LOT, a lot, a lot!

It means everything to do with your vital dynamic (or not) life force, your internal drive and mojo - how old you feel and how energised you are each and every morning.

Life's events have given us plenty of opportunities to awaken in our consciousness - to become self-aware in healthy ways. To grow up! Did you know that the energy systems in your own body have the capacity to develop in you more harmony and balance, particularly if you know how to feed them on all levels.

Firstly, before I continue, I have a few questions for you.

Let's pretend you are coming to see me as you are reading this. Almost the first question I will ask you is this:-

"What do you want to see, feel, and experience has changed significantly in three months from now, on a Mind, Body and Spirit level?"

Write down your answers - this is about your internal engine, and we are taking an MOT of yourself.

It's no use having the money to retire, for instance, if you are not well, depleted and not even sleeping refreshingly. Believe me, many people's lives are exactly like that.

Let's take a sober yet gentle look at your true energy state.

- Are you honestly one of the walking dead inside yourself, and if not now, when is the time to reverse what you don't like?
- Retirement from what was one chapter of your life, is an exciting time to get yourself in the best shape ever, and on all levels, not just physical.

Life seems to dictate that we live from the outside to impact the inside. In fact, though, our own spiritual essence, soul (not religious) and our own maturing sexuality literally longs for us to live with increasing awareness of the depth and breadth of being fully human. Simply that means living the other way around.

INSIDE TO OUTSIDE!

When we don't, we are propelled into thinking there is something wrong as we become increasingly depleted.

That is what is RIGHT with you - it is a clever sign from your own Integrated being that it is time to pay attention to your **inside life force – the batteries that really run the show!**

Our life force is ignited from within us - not from the outside.

RETIREMENT from one chapter, almost like any other event or thing you want to achieve, needs to be prepared for so that you gain maximum from the next experience.

Challenges, transitions or changing chapters in your life will automatically bring up the next layer of signposts to unravel more of your own unique potential to be vibrantly alive, energised and at peace in dynamic ways. Even with health challenges, you can remain intact and well in your behaviours, choices and attitudes.

These are some of the questions that I would ask you, so do yourself a favour – write them down, as that will facilitate more choices about how to retire well.

Sit comfortably, shut off all other distractions. Take a few deep breaths, observing your answers with respect and care.

- Do you consider yourself to be fully awake to your life-force – comfortable in your own skin, mind, body and spirit?
  Are you able to be the person that you like to wake up with?!
- How well do you feel on each level, Mind, Body and Spirit? Think of them as your internal bank accounts. What shape are they in – full and with compound interest accumulating as a metaphor, or bankrupt and with no spare anything anywhere?

- Are you sharp and alert on many different levels simultaneously?
- Have you managed to get out of the trap of only identifying yourself as your job, your title, your marital status, your children's achievements, or not, the sum of money you have in your bank?
- Or are you catching yourself 'owning' insidiously your high cholesterol, arthritis or lack of fitness as if they are just simply signs of your age? Which you apparently feel you are powerless over?
- Are you cutting corners because you can, but you're scared, deeply, inside by your thinning hair, your thickening waistline, your lack of memory recall?
- Are you joining in with the noise that is so prevalent around us about our apparent lack of choice when it comes to all sorts of dis-eased states.
- Are you booking, with anxiety, your jabs for shingles, flu etc, without really looking at what on earth you are really doing with your own precious life?
- Are you able to stop handing over your health's needs to others and fully participate, be self-centred (rather than self-absorbed) in a way that makes you able to 'BE PRESENT' to your own needs? Let alone others' needs?

Allow yourself to review your answers later.

Vibrant Integrated health is not necessarily the absence of signs and symptoms, but it is about your own relationship with yourself, in Mind, Body and Spirit.

The bridge between your Mind, Body and Spirit is the maturing of your sexuality and your spirituality. Traditional Medicine always focuses on your own life force and energy systems.

As the internal systems in your body develop and with increasing consciousness on your part, you have far more choice about how your own energy operates. It is a massive change to begin to know that the following will impact your own sense of real well-being. A Traditional Integrated Medical practitioner will show you how to use all your human capacities, keeping your organs balanced for each chapter that arises.

What does that look like : -

1. Being present to listen, be curious, enjoy all aspects of life, including the need to be available to yourself and others.

2. Having strong senses of your own worth, but in humility. You become more interested in others than in yourself, as it has become a healthy habit to take responsibility for your own well-being, so that you are automatically available to others.

3. Knowing yourself well and having some sort of discipline around what really works for you and what doesn't, prioritising your own growth, goals and intentions.

4. Emotionally being flexible and in charge of yourself, and no longer, let's say, being such a hothead!

5. You no longer run from what you are feeling and are not so easily triggered by people, places or events. Equally you know damn well when you are distracting yourself and avoiding some painful aspects of what faces most of us, often in life. You stop yourself, for instance, from getting involved in another relationship before you have taken the time to work out why the last one didn't work.!?

6. You have weathered so many storms that you know your strengths and have started to master your fragilities.

7. You know how to make love to life itself - what does that look like - as an example a taxi driver is exceptionally rude and aggressive so instead of reacting and letting his stuff ruin your day you relax and take the time to pay his fare and then ask him if there is anything going on. Mostly, he or she would be surprised that you were showing a kind aspect of our humanity. His response could be, and in one real occasion that I was involved in, his shoulders relaxed as he slumped into the utter misery of what was to come out of his mouth next. His wife died a week earlier, and he did not know what to do with himself except go back to work, but of course, he was not really in a fit state to be at work. After listening intently for some time, he had cried and let go of some of his deep grief, and of course, was no longer aggressive.

8. You now know that to listen deeply, is the solution so often. You are no longer constantly trying to fix people. You certainly know not to bully, judge and shame them.

9. You realise we are here to love one another, to accept, not necessarily here to like!

10. You have absolutely understood that what you put out in life sooner or later boomerangs back at you.

11. You know how to influence your world with your choice of attitude and behaviour, but you equally have learnt that control just ultimately backfires!

12. You accept what you realise you cannot change, and you are wise enough to only change what you can.

The concept of living comfortably in the web of the sexual and spiritual life force is:

1. **Becoming more aware of the depth and breadth of being a human spirit or soul in a physical body. WHICH deeply embodies the knowledge that we are all one in our very essence.** There simply is not the separation that we have believed, so to become aware of what the 'oneness' means is simply getting that we cannot live as an island that is only in service to itself - we are love at our deepest core. We can have a bow wave of energy that makes the world a better place, and particularly for those who are not yet awake.

2. You have discovered who you are, who you are not and what is propelling you out of your bed every day. What your priorities are, and importantly, you are no longer necessarily driven by your physical body's needs, only! Or your intellectual ones either.

3. There are so many times in our lives that we must put off spending more time with the people, places and things that really do float our boat, but we are able to handle it with Grace and not take it out on all those around us.

4. We are far more patient and wiser.

5. We have a sense of the ridiculous and do not take life seriously, even though of course, it is.

6. Far less reactivity as you fundamentally get that we are not less than, more than, but equal to - in other words, you live in an awareness of how vital it is that you understand and live forgiving yourself and others continually. None of us is behaving in the ideal ways that we would like.

7. You can mean and say that you are sorry for your part in something that has caused another pain - you know how to make amends in a way that would serve the other and not just your own ego!

8. Far more actions instead, as we choose to be a part of the solutions rather than responding with groaning, moaning our way through the endless streams of problems that just do arise.

9. Far more knowledge, grounded in experience.

10. We don't mind making a fool of ourselves.

11. As the weaving continues but gets stronger, our own life force can become so much more dynamic as we are using both our sexuality and our spirituality to be in our world. In the West, the mere word sexuality triggers all sorts of associations that are not actually relevant to this concept. The Porn industry is an indicator of how complex and misunderstood this powerful force is in our world. **To be tamed and understood is one of the many internal voyages a human needs to go on to become more settled in themselves.** It is one of the founding concepts of Traditional Medicine in the East and Spiritual Truths around the world.

12. A simplistic way of looking at this huge concept is that initially as we grow into our own individual sexuality and what it means to us it is mostly a physical concept, and only later as we mature it becomes a more emotional and spiritual reality which is woven into all our human aspects - Mind, Body and Spirit.

13. We have usually discovered where we are with hand-me-down concepts of faith in something larger than

ourselves, so we have usually developed a dialogue and discipline around something that feeds us internally. Meditation, prayer, martial arts, art, gardening, walking - the choice is huge.

14. Our self-respect and inner knowing means that we automatically find ways of renewing and cleansing our own systems on physical levels as well as the other aspects of ourselves.

Review your own answers and see where you really are. Allow yourself the incredible and courageous adventure of unhooking yourself from what does not serve your mind, body and spirit any longer. Expand what does so that you oversee your life force, igniting your own inner bank accounts with compound interest and not depletion.

Allow this to be the next best chapter of your precious life.

Catherine Rolt

International best-selling Author
and Integrated Chinese Medical Consultant

With 40 years of clinical experience in Eastern Medicine and being a patient of both Western & Eastern Medicine myself, I have a unique outlook on what makes Integrated Health so important to us all, no matter our challenges or what each chapter of our precious lives is looking like. Treating not only your symptoms but your mind, body and soul can be the difference between thriving and just surviving. As soon as we understand the point of our struggles, challenges, differing stages of life and even our pains, we can be steering, rather than have ourselves steered!

Catherine Rolt Book Links on Amazon

- The Slipstream To The Miraculous
- UnRavel Dis-Ease Naturally: Season by Season
- The Pain Paradox: How Pain Can Lead to Inner Peace and Lightness of Being

CatherineARolt.com

Not Retired, Not Late, Not Lazy—Just Wired Differently, Even Now

Louise Baker

I'm recovering from a migraine, brought on by a period of intense work and an inspiring brain conference—and suddenly, my words have disappeared. I feel obsessive and fatigued, and nothing feels quite right. I begin to wonder: is this a medical issue? Is this brain fog and forgetfulness the onset of dementia?

Or is it something else?

Despite my therapeutic training, I wasn't prepared for how this would feel. I know our experiences are shaped by internal drivers and context. Still, I wasn't expecting this moment of collapse.

To explain, I need to tell my story.

For years, I worked in corporate life—selling tech, managing vending machines and technical products, even patrolling London's streets as a police officer. I've worked for both large blue-chip companies and smaller organisations, and I've been self-employed. I was mostly an individual contributor, winning performance awards, later becoming a manager. Then I made a shift—stepping out of the corporate rhythm and into a quieter life.

I opened a therapeutic practice offering Hypnotherapy and NLP. It gave me space to think, feel, and offer others the same. Eventually, after years of managing properties, caretaking for ageing parents and pets, and volunteering, I pursued a Master's degree in neuroscience and the psychology of mental health.

If I'd known how hard it would be, I might not have started. Was it my age? The wear and tear of life?

The degree felt like torture. I worked hard, but academic writing was a battle. I couldn't produce essays with flow. Multiple-choice tests left me drained and doubting myself. My husband gently asked why I found it so hard. I began to fear cognitive decline.

Then one day, my academic supervisor asked to speak with me. What she said changed everything.

She told me that when we spoke, I grasped and applied ideas at a high level. But my essays read as if written by someone else. They lacked flow and connection. I wasn't doing myself justice. She suggested I be assessed for dyslexia.

At 56, I was diagnosed as quite dyslexic – not in the way most people imagine. I can read, but only if it's something that truly interests me. I've never been able to force myself to read what I didn't enjoy. Fortunately, much of the Master's content fascinated me, so I could focus on those parts.

After the diagnosis, I revisited my school and work history. Supervisors often described my writing as tired or inconsistent. But no one ever asked why. No one thought to suggest a different way of thinking.

Looking back, I saw how I had unconsciously or cleverly avoided roles requiring writing. I crafted a career around speaking, summarising, and contributing verbally. I always worked with someone who could write on my behalf. That's called adaptation.

So why does this matter now?

Because when people who have thrived in structured careers retire, the scaffolding that has quietly supported their identity and function can disappear. And if you don't realise it was there, its absence can feel like a personal collapse.

That's what this is really about: scaffolding, and why it matters – especially in retirement.

In both neuroscience and psychology, scaffolding refers to the mental constructs that shape identity, structure, and function. Throughout our careers, we build strong neural frameworks: habits, patterns, responses. The brain comes to "know" who you are and what you're meant to be doing. It becomes efficient in those roles.

And then… you retire.

Let's look at the neuroscience for a moment.

Our brains are built from densely packed neurons, forming networks that manage how we process, store, and retrieve information. Different networks govern different processes. For instance, the default mode network reflects on memory and internal thoughts, while the executive network handles focus and decision-making.

These systems shape how we move through the world – and how we see ourselves.

Over time, repetitive routines build predictive structures. The brain becomes a master of efficiency. It anticipates what comes next based on what has come before.

When the familiar patterns vanish, we lose more than our

schedules –we lose a part of how our brain understands who we are.

The result? You might feel confused, adrift, even frightened. Your mind may seem slower. Memories may fade. And if you don't understand what's happening, it's easy to fear the worst.

But what's happening is often not degeneration – maybe it's re-scaffolding.

When you retire or experience a major life change, your brain must reorganise. If you haven't prepared mentally, emotionally, or neurologically, this period can feel like a crisis. But really, it's your brain clearing the decks and asking: What do we do now?

That can feel like noise. But it's just a brain adapting.

This shift is even harder if you're neurodivergent.

My dyslexia—and my compulsive fascination with new ideas—made this process more acute. Later in life, I learned I also had traits associated with ADHD, particularly something called compensatory overworking. It explained a lot. As a child, I was obsessed with dinosaurs but couldn't remember their names. My brother strategised with money in board games; I chased the excitement of the game and just moved it around.

Over time, I've learned to recognise when I'm lost in tangents, overwhelmed by detail, or overly focused. I've learned to apply neuroscience strategies to my own wellbeing—and now I encourage others to do the same, especially in retirement.

Here's why. When you stop working, you lose more than your job. You lose external cues: waking up for meetings, submitting reports, even the coffee queue. And you don't realise how much these rhythms held your identity in place.

Your brain doesn't like chaos. It seeks certainty. If you don't replace old routines with new ones, it tries to take you back. This creates dissonance—mental friction. You feel unsettled, unsure of your purpose. You begin to ask: *Who am I now?*

And if you've never consciously considered that before, it can be deeply unsettling.

In an increasingly secular society, many of the old anchors of purpose – faith, tradition, even stable community – have loosened. Retirement forces you to create your own framework.

If you don't do that work, your brain fills in the gaps with discomfort.

Let's be clear: the brain is a mechanism. A wonderful, adaptive, living one. And it needs care.

You may have heard of myelin sheathing – the insulation around your brain's wiring. When that breaks down, cognitive functions can slow or fragment. Myelin is vital for memory, learning, and clarity. But its health depends on inputs: nutrition, movement, sleep, hydration.

If your cognitive load increases – say, from stress or emotional fatigue – and your brain isn't nourished, you enter what I call invisible collapse. Things take longer. Energy fades. You feel overwhelmed by tasks that once felt easy.

This is normal. But it can be frightening.

One cause of invisible collapse is losing the coping mechanisms you didn't know you had. A professional qualification, for instance, might have masked a neurodivergence for decades. Take away that structure, and suddenly your strategies are exposed. That's what happened to me when I began my Master's.

I had to write. I couldn't avoid it. And I struggled. Not with ideas—those I had plenty of – but with flow. With finding the right words. I realised how cleverly I had built a life around avoiding writing.

And that understanding was freeing.

It made sense of the things I'd blamed myself for. And it made me passionate about helping others understand their brains, too – especially during life transitions like retirement.

If you're approaching that phase, I urge you to invest in therapy, coaching, or self-reflection. These aren't indulgences. They're tools for re-scaffolding your life.

Had I understood this earlier, it would have made a world of difference. Knowing that my brain isn't broken – just different – was a huge relief. Forgetting names, losing momentum, or panicking about purpose isn't a distressing diagnosis. It's a signal that something is shifting.

And the good news? The brain is neuroplastic. It can rebuild.

With care, intention, and a bit of neuroscience, you can help your brain lay new scaffolding. You can create new routines, new purposes, and new stories. You can reinvent how you show up in the world.

Of course, be vigilant. If something doesn't feel right, seek advice. Red flags like sudden confusion, personality change, or getting lost in familiar places need attention. But don't jump to the worst-case scenario. Sometimes it's not dementia. Sometimes, it's disruption.

And disruption can be a doorway to growth.

So notice what shows up.

Accept support. Ask for help—yes, even practice being a burden. Don't wait until the wheels fall off.

If you're dyslexic or neurodivergent, know that your wiring is just different. If your life has changed suddenly – retirement, relocation, grief – remember that your brain is adjusting. It's not malfunctioning. It's trying to make sense of a new reality.

It needs your help.

So build new scaffolding. Be kind to yourself. Keep learning. Keep asking questions.

And above all, remember: this is your brain, transitioning – not degenerating or disappearing.

About Louise Baker

Louise Baker MSc brings a warm, neuroscience-informed approach to mindset, wellbeing, and personal growth. With forty-plus years of experience as a therapist and commercial practitioner, she combines scientific insight with deep empathy. She currently focuses on neuroplasticity and AI with *joinvital.ai*, and delivering *whileiwait.uk* – a programme supporting people facing long waits for diagnoses, scans, or treatments, including those with brain tumours.

Louise understands the emotional toll of uncertainty and uses neuroscience to create practical, accessible tools for resilience. A lifelong learner living with dyslexia, she models the same growth mindset she helps others develop. Clients describe her as both grounding and inspiring, helping them reconnect with inner strength, focus, and the capacity to grow — even in difficult circumstances.

Louise's mission is simple: To help people shine, even through life's hardest moments.

linkedin.com/in/louisebaker

https://www.facebook.com/louisebakeruk

https://www.instagram.com/touch_works

https://joinvital.ai

https://whileiwait.uk

When It Feels Like The Beginning Of The End... Some Forget To Live—Others Choose To Forget To Grow Old. The Choice Is Yours.

Menno Siebinga

"I've worked hard my whole life. So that I can eventually retire and do the things I love, and now that I'm almost there, I see those very things becoming out of reach." Ria 67-year-old client

Ria, her situation is unfortunately not uncommon, but does that have to be the case?

It was like she was working hard aboard the Titanic—making life better for everyone else, hoping her time to enjoy the journey would come later. Some question the comparison because the Titanic ended tragically. But this isn't about the sinking—it's about the warning signs we see but ignore until the life we were working toward starts slipping away, causing unnecessary damages and loss (of quality) of life.

The fact is, we are all going to hit an iceberg eventually; that's something we cannot prevent. However, we can avoid not having the time of our lives and hitting it unnecessarily or too early.

The Iceberg of Unnecessary Decline

For most people, life begins like the Titanic leaving harbour—in peak condition and full of big dreams and promises. However, as we age, predictable changes occur: muscle mass decreases, and stamina declines. Many people are aware of this, but not enough act on it. They fool themselves into thinking they're doing enough of the right things.

Ria was playing tennis three times a week. She believed it was enough. But deep down, she knew it wasn't. That's what I call the iceberg of unnecessary decline.

The Titanic didn't miss the iceberg—they saw it. But it was too late to turn. Likewise, you can't expect to stay in shape by doing the same things over time.

The first thing I learned in physiotherapy school was: "Function forms structure." If you repeat the same routine, you will still slowly decline. But when you challenge your body, it adapts. It's not use it or lose it—it's challenge it or lose it.

Start by pushing just 4% beyond what feels possible. That's always possible. Combine that with smart recovery, and your body will respond effectively.

A Small Fall, A Big Consequence

Five years ago, Ria had a minor fall that had significant consequences. Many problems that come with ageing, like losing the ability to do what we love, often start small. From that moment, her mobility and strength began to decline.

Nine months ago, her knee and Achilles started hurting badly. Walking became difficult. And what began as a minor stumble ended in the sinking realisation: "I'm degenerating."

The life she had envisioned after retiring—hiking the Scottish Highlands, playing tennis, travelling with her partner—felt like it was slipping away.

Physiotherapy didn't help the way she'd hoped.

She kept moving—because that's what we're told: "Stay active, or you'll decline." But movement alone isn't the answer, especially if it's painful or misaligned. It's like driving a car with a broken engine. You may be moving, but are you going forward—or slowly breaking down?

Even elite athletes, with all the support in the world, get sidelined by injuries—not from impact, but from ineffective use that goes unnoticed, repeated over time, and paired with insufficient recovery. Eventually, this leads to breakdown instead of adaptation. Ageing is similar.

We often think life and ageing wear us down—when, in reality, it's how we use our bodies that hold us back.

Many of the challenges we associate with ageing are like the injuries athletes face: not inevitable, but often preventable. We play the game of life, but too often, we play it in ways that feel good in the moment—despite knowing better—costing us the ability to keep playing well over a lifetime.

What Doctors Often Miss

Recently, I spoke with a client in her 50s who was experiencing hip pain. Her doctor said, "It's arthrosis—learn to live with it." He assumed: You're already 50; this is just how your body is now.

But she thought I didn't want to be confined by this. I'm only 50. I still want to do so many things.

She had to ask herself to be referred to the hospital for pictures.

We had an online consultation and were able to give her direct advice on how to create the right circumstances to walk and move pain-free again. We could see the deficiencies she had in her left hip and leg compared to the right, as well as how she was using and maintaining them differently.

I often see this – clients are told to accept it as part of the ageing process. Yes, we all decline. But how – and how quickly – is primarily up to us.

When I asked if the pain was constant, she said, "Sometimes yes, sometimes no."

If you can move without pain for one second, you can have two. Then three. We have to figure out how. I've seen many people accept their situation as unfixable – but we've helped them do the things that make them feel alive again.

Ria's Story: From Decline to Determination

Ria, at first, was accepting her fate—she was declining, and her dream of walking through the Scottish Highlands was fading and closing like a sunset. Beautiful, but slowly slipping away.

Then something switched. She thought, "This can't go on."

That moment was her iceberg. Her signal. Her SOS.

She thought of me and booked an appointment. Just before her session, while shaving her legs, she noticed how much smaller one calf was compared to the other. She could now see she was really deteriorating, and something had to happen.

Not having cancelled her dream holiday to Scotland yet, and

it was just five weeks away. Her husband wasn't looking forward to it, thinking he'd be travelling with "two older people and a disabled wife."

After a few sessions, things began to shift. She could walk farther—without pain. She felt like she was regaining traction in life.

On the trip, she walked 10 kilometres—pain-free.

She returned, thinking, "I want to play tennis again. Try padel."

She even started going to the gym—something she never imagined doing. Within two weeks, she already felt a difference.

What amazed me most was that she began inspiring others. On the phone with her brother, who was heading to visit a sick friend, she shared her story—showing that change can still happen, and even quickly.

For her, what felt behind her became something she could do again. Not just once—but as often as she chose.

One Decision Away

There are two key points I would like to make.

First, I don't define vitality as something you either have or don't. I define it as your ability to make better decisions in any situation.

More vitality or getting a grip on your vitality is then just one decision away. That makes being on track to vitality attainable, even when you're desperate and/or out of shape. It shows us where to focus on. That's what Ria did. She didn't choose to fall—but she decided how to respond.

We often say you have to accept how things are.

But that doesn't mean you have to accept they'll stay that way. Ria thought tennis three times a week was enough. It wasn't. She saw it. And she responded.

Second: She had lifelines all along.

Pain. Shrinking muscle. A gut feeling.

But only when she truly faced it did she take action. And that action changed everything—just weeks before retirement. Her future no longer looked like a fading sunset. It looked like a sunrise.

Becoming a Superager

This is what I call a Superager.

Someone who knows they're ageing but chooses to make the most of it.

Someone focused on building vitality freedom—the way others create financial freedom.

Someone who raises the bar of what we believe is possible as we age.

Superagers take action and enjoy themselves for the benefit of tomorrow, not at the expense of tomorrow. They choose to challenge themselves just 4% beyond what feels easy, so daily movement becomes effortless—not exhausting. They listen to SOS signals. They don't ignore the warning signs or write them off as "just getting older."

Ria is on her way to becoming a Superager now.

She goes to the gym. She does the work. She's reclaiming joy, strength, and possibility.

Not long ago, her daily movements were filled with pain and effort.

Now, they feel like life is moving forward and becoming effortless.

Rather Die (Or Decline) Than Ask For Help.

One big reason people don't take the lifeline is mental. I saw this in myself – absurdly, in hindsight.

In my mid-twenties, after graduating from physiotherapy school, I was on a world trip. I'd just taught capoeira on a beach in Java, Indonesia, and decided to swim – still mentally in Thailand, where the sea was calm. This beach had a strong current.

Suddenly, I couldn't get back. I was in danger. Then I saw the father of one of my students, off duty, walking by. He was the head lifeguard, and he was waving at me.

Life offered me a lifeline

And what did I do.....

I did nothing.

I was too ashamed to ask for help. Too afraid of what he might think.

I was drowning, not because I couldn't be saved – but because I didn't take the lifeline right in front of me.

The Two Best Times To Act

I see this all the time – people sense something is off but hesitate to ask for help. They make excuses, even when they know better.

As a result, they decline. Deteriorate. Stop doing the things they love.

There are two crucial moments to act if you want more vitality and a better return on life:

Early and Now.

Early means before your daily life is affected. Like checking your physical and mental "bank account" – knowing what you have, what you spend, and what you'll have if you keep going this way.

The easiest way to start is to take the Superagers Assessment, which we have developed specifically for this purpose. It takes 5 minutes to complete and immediately gives you an idea of how you score on the five skills we have found to be present in Superagers. Visit *https://superagers.scoreapp.com/* to take this free assessment.

Now means listening when your body sends signals. Don't ignore them and give them a chance to grow, as they may have a bigger, unwanted impact on your life. Adjust how you move, be honest about what's missing, and get support to build the skills you lack– before a minor issue becomes a big one.

One Decision Away

We often say people must accept what's happening—but that doesn't mean you have to admit that it stays this way.

Ria didn't. And eventually, neither did I.

In that water in Indonesia, I stopped fighting the current and swam toward a nearby surfer. Using hands and gestures – I barely spoke the language – I asked if I could hold onto his board.

That day, I survived. But a part of my ego didn't.

The part that thought pride would keep me safe... almost cost me everything.

That moment in the water taught me something I never forgot:

Sometimes, the only thing standing between survival and thriving, or suffering is the willingness to ask for help.

Vitality is like that.

It's not just about muscle or mindset - it's about making better decisions. And the courage to move forward. Even if it's just 4% more than you think you can. Even if it's just one more rep. One better habit. One braver conversation.

You are not too old. It is not too late. And you're not done yet

Remember: One decision. That's all it takes to start unlocking vitality – and your most significant return on life.

May the choice be with you.

About Menno Siebinga

Menno Siebinga is a Longevity Trainer and Superager Coach committed to helping people over 50 unlock new levels of vitality, strength, and purpose—often beyond what they believed possible. A former physiotherapist, Menno's path was shaped by caring for his mother during a debilitating neurological illness, an experience that revealed society's blind spots about ageing and potential.

In response, he developed a mission to challenge outdated beliefs about what's possible later in life. Today, he helps clients transform into Superagers—from a 91-year-old walking unaided to a 58-year-old achieving peak physical and cognitive performance.

Menno envisions a world where people invest in their "vitality fund" as seriously as their pension—so ageing becomes an empowering chapter, not a slow decline.

Through his coaching, Menno shows people how to "forget to grow old" and live fully, regardless of age or circumstance—proving it's never too late to reclaim your energy, purpose, and joy.

www.bodyenbrein.nl

www.superagers.com

Facebook and LinkedIn

superagers.com

Rollercoaster Or Walk In The Park: Your Choice

Lathizile Dube

Retirement, which is the act of withdrawing from one's occupation or position, upon reaching a certain age (though an inevitable part of anyone's working life), is one of the most significant transitions that you can go through, but one of the least thought-through. To put yourself in the position where you allow the governmental or organisational cut-off age to be your horizon, sets you up for a rude awakening and has associated risks. People usually fall into, but are not limited to, three broad categories when it comes to retirement.

- You plan carefully for retirement at a specific time (this differs from the mandated retirement age) and what you will do after retirement.
- You may experience retirement as a result of the profession you're in or the age cut-off (on-time retirement).
- Retirement that creeps up on you early, and it is necessary to step back from your work (sudden retirement).

Regardless of which category you fall into, navigating this process is essential. Sewdas R, de Wind A, Stenholm S, et al (2020);74:473-480 Association between retirement and mortality: working longer, living longer? A systematic review and meta-analysis, Epidemiol Community Health, concluded that "early retirement was not associated with a higher risk of mortality. On-time retirement was associated with a higher risk of mortality, which might reflect the healthy worker effect." This conclusion was drawn from a total of 25 separate studies conducted in Europe. This risk is statistically higher for men, as their self-definition, worth, and ability to provide are often entangled in their career or work. This impacts everyone around them as it may be a barrier to genuine connection.

There is life after retirement; you must put yourself in a position to make the best possible transition as you step into this new season. Acknowledging that retirement is a transition into a different phase of life is critical for you to handle the various aspects of the transition effectively. It is a shift, not a change, although there will be changes during the process of transitioning into retirement.

Several mental and practical steps can ease the transition and enable you to enjoy a fulfilling and prosperous life after leaving a professional career or occupation, or stepping away from a role.

Each step requires you to be intentionally present in your experience to maximise the benefits of the life process you are going through.

What this looks like practically is noticing how you feel and what thoughts come up for you in a given stage. (The following stages do not happen in a specific order, and some will last through the whole transition and run concurrently with another stage.)

The stages are:

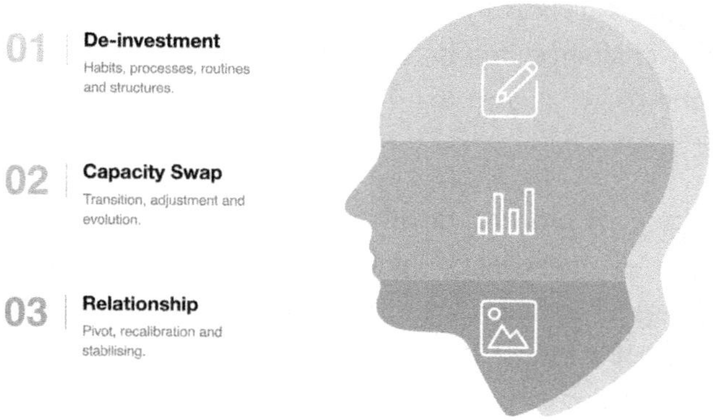

De-investment

When in the working phase of life, most of the processes, routines and structures are centred around work and how to be more productive and obtain the necessary outputs and deliverables for one's job or occupation or role. These habits, processes, systems, and structures are implemented over years, if not decades, and done in a way that you may not be aware of how work-centred your life may be.

Once this phase is over, there is a need for deliberate deconstruction, a process that should be as intentional and thought-through as one's working life was. There are the obvious things that will cease at retirement: you will no longer be required to show up at your workplace or interact with your colleagues to engage in work; you will no longer have to be up-to-date with your projects, clients, or responsibilities that pertain to your role. There are also less considered attributes to consider, such as the emotional attachment to it all: your colleagues, the identity or profession, the status associated with your role or organisation, and the physical routines and structures built around showing up and being available.

Deconstructing the practical parts when retirement is approaching is relatively straightforward. What is hard and where the challenge lies is how to disassemble the emotional attachment to what you are leaving, and this is where people often get stuck.

In the case of emotional detachment, you need to undergo the process of decathect, which is the process of withdrawing one's feelings of attachment from a person, idea or object, as in anticipation of a future loss. This can be done after retirement, but it is a conscious process that will allow you to retire well. It means you can choose how to withdraw and disconnect from that which is now over, while honouring the work you have done over the decades and what that has meant to you and your experience. This process is essential before you retire as it smooths out the transition and allows you to have autonomy as you move ahead.

Capacity Swap

As you retire, a significant amount of capacity becomes available in your life, resulting from the transition.

People choose to fill this gap in different ways; some take on board positions advising on the industry or role they have left, while others fill it with hobbies and interests that they did not have time for in the working world.

The family now takes on a bigger role, as there is the capacity to include more of those dear ones who have always been close by or not. All of these are very good as they give something to look forward to, and this is a healthy way to cultivate hope in the future. One thing that can empower you to do well in this process and not hit the wall of proverbial emptiness is to allow the process to evolve naturally.

What that means in real terms is to enable the capacity created through retirement to be filled naturally with what comes along, when a void is created somewhere. This may cause tension and mixed emotions, but allowing yourself to sit back and reflect on your retirement experience, you allow yourself to adjust and be open and flexible to the opportunities that are naturally around you.

This process may take from 6 months to 18 months to enable your experience to evolve as you decide what you want to engage in and how you would like it to impact and affect your life.

Relationship

Relationships are the foundation of life, as no one is an island, and the quality of your relationships is crucial for navigating the transition into retirement. All the significant life transitions we must navigate in this life will be based on our relationships, and we need to consider the order of significance to understand what needs to be done.

The relationships closest to you, such as those with your significant other and close family members, will likely change as a result of retirement. You may have a partner who is younger and is still working when you are off work, and you may not have been present in sharing the mental load. Many find themselves unprepared for the amount of time they suddenly have on their hands, which can lead to feelings of despondency.

Accepting that significant adjustments will be required internally upon retirement is essential. The adjustments start with you, as you are the one shifting. It is unrealistic to impose your discomfort and tension on those close to you, as nothing may have changed for them.

You do not want to alienate them in your initial frustration inadvertently. Be prepared to navigate confusion and frustration at the beginning of this shift, particularly in relationships.

Allowing time to process, journaling and seeking the right support will help you to strengthen your relationships rather than the opposite.

Men suddenly find themselves in a foreign, familiar place that can be bewildering. The dynamics change entirely once retirement arrives because you have more time on your hands and now have to redefine your systems structure and processes in ways that become more home-centred. This can be a painful shift if you don't have a solid relationship with your partner and have used work as an excuse to avoid dealing with critical issues. Many men find the process humbling, as their authority is no longer based on provision and must be derived from the input in the relationships they have chosen to have with those close to them.

As mentioned previously, give yourself time to find your new place of equilibrium in this new phase of life. This requires recalibration with your significant other and addressing the challenges and barriers that may prevent a deep, meaningful relationship. Stabilising the immediate family dynamics will allow the rest of your retirement journey to run a lot smoother than allowing chaos and dysfunction to persist. New routines, systems, and rhythms will be established through these core relationships, allowing you to welcome more into your life.

A grounded friendship that you nurture and draw from is a place where the richness of your retirement experience will be palpable. Being intentional about how you want to interact with and engage with your friendships is a crucial consideration, whether through sports, hobbies, volunteering, clubs, or areas of interest. This allows you to remain relevant and seen in ways that enable you to achieve your new happiness gradually.

Through the support of good friends, you can see your perspective and live variably through their experiences, while offering the wealth of knowledge and experience you have accumulated over your lifetime.

Seeking out new friendships with people of different ages, particularly those younger, is essential, as it allows you to relate to multiple generations and avoid isolation.

Every retirement journey is different and should be tailored to your specific needs and requirements. These stages above may be essential for some and surplus to requirements for others. Some stages occur concurrently for some, while others may have distinct intervals. The process is overall continuous, so revisiting the stages is advisable to achieve the best results. The beauty of the retirement transition is that it is a transition you can make with a wealth of experience and knowledge behind you, unlike other significant life transitions.

Therefore, take the time to be intentional about the process.

About Lathizile Dube

Lathizile Dube has over a decade and a half of dedicated refinement on her craft. The methodologies she created and employed have redefined the landscape of human optimisation and transformational change. Lathi focuses on transitions of an upward nature within organisations across global industries. Lathi has honed her skills, techniques and methodologies through education and experience working with individuals as well as groups. Her unwavering belief in unlocking the full potential of individuals underscores every facet of her work. Lathi has an evident and concise approach, with the unique ability to translate complex frameworks and ideas into simple, digestible parts. With her experience as a member of Therapy Harley Street, where she sees clients one-on-one, she can harness her deep understanding of the human psyche to inform the work she does powerfully. Lathi thrives in complex and challenging multicultural environments, where her vast skill set comes into its own.

https://calendly.com/lathi/id-consult?month=2025-07

Rewire Before You Retire

Amanda Hart

I remember walking into the kitchen the day after my mother retired, to see her standing at the kitchen window watching her neighbours leaving in their cars to go to work. I felt her subtle panic, the tangible feeling of her recognition that her world had changed and she was suddenly no longer part of the life she'd known for decades. The people, the meaning, the schedules.

She cried and told me her life now had no value, she was isolated, no one needed her, and she didn't know what her purpose was anymore. Amplified by the fact that she had just lost her mother, my grandmother, she was starkly aware that she was not only an 'orphan' as she put it but had no function in her life. It was like she had dropped off the edge of the world into another one that was alien to her.

I've witnessed this firsthand, both in my own life and in the lives of my clients. Time and again, the emotional challenges of the empty nest, menopause, and retirement have surfaced. Retirement often unfolds not as people imagine it would, filled with travel, family time, new hobbies, or long-awaited learning. Instead, I came to understand that retirement often brings just as many challenges, if not more, especially when people are suddenly faced with a half-empty planner and a loss of structure.

The absence of routine can feel disorienting, leaving many to question their identity and purpose.

The question, *"What now?"* asked into a quiet morning cup of tea is much more than something to contemplate on our to do list of wishes and desires. Retirement, for many, comes wrapped in paradox… longed for and feared in equal measure. After years of routine, role-playing, and responsibility, the space that opens up can feel unsettling.

But what I've witnessed and learned over many years, and now firmly believe, is that retirement isn't about withdrawal, it's about return… a return to self, to soul, to curiosity. It's a rite of passage as sacred as birth or falling in love… if we let it be.

I've spent decades guiding people through life's most tender transitions – divorce, grief, trauma recovery, the loss of identity. Retirement, it turns out, carries all of those threads. There's grief for what's over. Fear of irrelevance. A craving for purpose. And underneath it all, a deep invitation to ask ourselves...

"Who am I now, when I don't have to be what the world expected?"

Retirement begins long before the pension kicks in. The first step is internal – a gentle but thorough rewiring of the mind. Many of us have unconsciously internalised the belief that aging means decline. We see youth as valuable, and elderhood as invisible. But that's a cultural myth, not a truth.

I encourage clients to begin a 30-day Emotional Detox before retirement. Each day, we pick one limiting belief to let go of such as *"I'm no longer useful. It's too late to start something new. People only care about what I used to do."* And we replace them with truths rooted in soul, such as *"I carry wisdom only time can teach. This is my time to create from freedom, not fear. I'm not done… I'm evolving."*

One woman I worked with had been a headteacher for over 40 years. Her calendar, wardrobe, and even self-worth was built around that role. When she retired, she felt like a ghost in her own home. We started with tiny rituals. She lit a candle every morning just for her. She made space in her wardrobe for clothes that made her feel playful. Eventually, she took up storytelling for children in hospital wards, something she'd dreamed of as a girl. This was not how she envisioned her retirement, but it came to her when she allowed herself time to adjust, breathe, allow her natural, creative, intuitive self to show her who she was and that led to the inspirations that started to shape a whole new life. New beginnings, new relationships, new purpose.

But for something new to arise in our life with the process of retirement, we need to learn the art of shedding. If you're feeling lost in retirement, it might be because you're still carrying everyone else's expectations, and this can be a common cause of disappointment loops.

I often guide people through a practice I call the Metaphorical Wardrobe Cleanse. We take inventory of the 'outfits' – the identities, roles, and beliefs you've been wearing and metaphorically, try them on again. For example 'the good parent'. Is it still serving you? Or 'the provider'. What happens if you let that go? And 'the self-sacrificer'. Is it time to trade it in?

We make space for new identities to emerge. Some might discover 'the curious explorer', 'the quiet artist', 'the elder guide,' or 'the joy seeker'.

Letting go isn't about loss. It's about making space for what's waiting to be born. From here you can create your soul résumé. You may have a wonderfully professional résumé, but your soul résumé is the one that matters most now. This lists the real accomplishments like the night you stayed with a friend through heartbreak, the times you chose love over fear, or the days you got out of bed when it was the last thing you wanted to do.

I encourage you to write this. Frame it. Own it. Because retirement doesn't diminish you... it finally frees you to live from your truth, rather than your titles.

Once you've reflected on the moments that you felt alive, free and really connected, you're ready to pack your Third Act Toolkit. In your third act, tools matter. But not spreadsheets and to-do lists – these are tools for the soul. Here are a few that I've worked with which have created life changing outcomes:

Legacy Letters

Write letters to the people who shaped you. These include mentors, friends, children, or even younger versions of yourself. Don't wait for your eulogy to be the moment people hear your heart. Share what they meant to you, how they helped shape your values, what you learned from them - big or small.

These letters become living legacies, expressions of gratitude, healing, and closure that ripple far beyond the page. Consider keeping a copy for yourself, as a reminder of the love and wisdom you've both given and received.

Soul Map

Draw a map of your life journey. Mark the turning point, both beautiful and brutal. What did each one teach you? Use colours, symbols, or dates to visualise your evolution. This practice isn't about nostalgia, it's about recognising the resilience, courage, and choices that brought you to now. Let this map guide your next chapter by showing you not just where you've been, but what your soul has been calling you toward all along.

Rewilding Journal

Start noticing what lights you up, not what you're good at, or what's useful, but what makes your cells hum, your body come alive, your heart sing. Write them down, even if they seem silly or impractical. Over time, you'll begin to see patterns - clues to your joy, your creativity, your most vital self. Rewilding is about reclaiming parts of you that may have been buried under responsibility. Let this journal be your permission slip to follow delight, not duty.

Curiosity Challenges

Try something totally unfamiliar that takes you out of your comfort zone, like pottery, salsa dancing, volunteering with teenagers, or growing mushrooms. Pick things that scare you just a little, excite you a lot, and stretch the edges of your identity. Retire your inner critic and become a beginner again. In doing so, you rewire your brain, awaken your spirit, and discover hidden gifts. Remember, play is not frivolous, it's sacred renewal for the soul.

Not every retirement needs to look like a cruise or gardening fest. You have permission to break the mould, and you can certainly let retirement bring out the rebel in you. Start a YouTube channel reading bedtime stories for youngsters. Host Elder Circles in your community, passing on lived wisdom… you don't need a title to share wisdom. Travel solo… not to escape, but to meet yourself in new landscapes. Mentor someone from a different generation… swap stories, not just advice.

One man I knew started painting at 68. He said, *"I stopped caring whether I was good. I just knew I'd been silent too long."* His work is now in local galleries, but more importantly, his soul is no longer on mute.

The hardest shift in retirement is often learning to simply be, the transitioning from 'doing' to 'being'. To sit with stillness, without needing to prove or produce. Stillness is where the soul speaks loudest, whether it's in meditation, on a long walk in nature or sitting quietly in your garden – stillness allows our intuitive, creative self to whisper to our heart's longing.

Practice what I call time alchemy. Instead of managing time, feel it. Don't schedule joy… follow it. You may find that in the spaces between tasks, your truest self starts whispering *"I've waited so long for you to come home."*

Retirement isn't about escape. It's not the end of relevance. It's a holy invitation to live aligned, possibly for the first time in decades. You are not done. You are returning… coming home to yourself.

You have been many things to many people. But now you get to be yours. Let your life become a poem, a patchwork, a wild and tender offering… not because you have to, but because you can.

Retirement, at its best, is less about retreating from life and more about reconnecting to the life inside you. So ask yourself gently, *"Who do I want to become, now that no one is watching? What would I do if I followed joy instead of duty? What part of me is waiting to be remembered?"*

The answers won't come all at once. But if you listen… really listen, retirement might just become your most meaningful, mischievous, and magical chapter yet.

About Amanda Hart

Amanda Hart is a trauma-informed transformational coach, author, and advocate for emotional recovery and personal reinvention. With over 30 years of experience in healing and hypnotherapy, she has trained under Dr. Keith Hearne, Paul McKenna and the pioneer Deborah Borgen. Her work integrates intuitive development and subconscious training through modalities such as the Silva Ultramind Method, which she has taught across the UK.

Amanda gained national recognition on *Britain's Psychic Challenge* and later became a media contributor, hosting *The Soul Searching Show* on radio and writing for *Soul & Spirit* and *Best Holistic Life* magazines. Her memoir, *The Guys Upstairs,* endorsed by Professor Evan Stark and other leading figures, explores trauma and coercive control with insight and authority.

She is the founder of *The Hub of Healing Hearts,* a gateway for survivors of narcissistic abuse, and an ambassador for philanthropist Andrew Dixon's See Through NPD. Amanda is currently producing a documentary film to inspire sustainable, systemic healing.

info@amanda-hart.co.uk

www.amanda-hart.co.uk

https://stan.store/AmandaHartHQ

YouTube: https://www.youtube.com/channel/UCtuhvjzA1xFc2FLLvpt1o9w

Facebook: https://www.facebook.com/AmandaHartHQ/

LinkedIn: https://www.linkedin.com/in/amandahart1/

Instagram: https://www.instagram.com/amandaharthq/

TikTok: https://www.tiktok.com/@authoramandahart

How to Retire

Jeff Buehner

My recommendations to anyone working toward retirement are typically broken into three categories.

- Advice given to young adults.
- Advice to middle-aged people and
- Advice to senior citizens.

I've never done things the conventional way. My way of doing things has worked for me and because my way is the only way I know, it's the only advice I'm able to offer.

That said. Follow it at your own risk.

The following is suited for any age. However, you may feel limited regarding how much of it you can implement depending on your age. It's a cold, hard reality that achieving the ability to retire comfortably is a race against the clock. The earlier you enter the race, the better your chances. No matter your age or how prepared you currently are, you can almost certainly retire with some level of dignity. No matter how old you are, it's time to buckle down and look at retirement as an essential and extremely important goal.

If you're already a senior citizen and don't feel prepared for retirement, don't despair. Read to the end for my final recommendation.

Recommendation #1: Pay Off A Home.

Owning a home free and clear is one of the best ways to cement your ability to retire comfortably when the time comes. Selling a paid-off, high-end home in a high-end neighborhood that's been appreciating for years almost guarantees a comfortable retirement somewhere.

One way to pay off your home is to focus like a laser on paying off something else first, like a car. Then put the money that used to go to that car payment toward eliminating the next payment. Once you have no other payments, put all the money into principle payments on your mortgage.

Surely, you waste enough money on luxuries and other non-essential items that you could, if you set your mind to it, eliminate a car payment. Get a head-start on it by selling that car and buying a less expensive used car. You may not look as good as your neighbor, but you'll revel in the knowledge that yours is paid for.

There's nothing like the feeling of being debt free! It's worth any sacrifice.

An expedited way to end up with a paid-off home, if you're suited to it, is to purchase and live in fixer-uppers. By updating the interior and beautifying the curb appeal of your home, combined with the natural appreciation that usually occurs, you should be able to sell that fixed up home at a profit. Roll your equity into buying another fixer upper. Each fixer-upper might be a little bigger and in a nicer neighborhood.

The equity checks you get upon selling each home should grow. If you do this successfully three or four times, you may be in the position to pay cash for your next fixer upper. Now, you're on your way!

Recommendation #2: Build A Profitable Business

The first and best asset anyone should strive to acquire is a profitable business. Sometimes a high-earning career qualifies. Owning a business that generates sufficient income to comfortably cover living expenses and provide a surplus, all but guarantees a comfortable retirement.

The earlier you get started the better. If you're focused and have forty years to find your niche, the odds of success are very high. If you only have five years before retirement, you can still do it.

Like selling a home, there's nothing like the feeling of selling a profitable business and walking away with a fat check.

Also, there's no law that says you must sell to retire. Consider hiring a manager or having one of your adult children manage your business. Another possibility is finding a young, motivated individual who you can take under your wing and train to manage the business with the goal of eventually owning it and buying you out over a fifteen-year contract. Better yet, have them go to the bank. Use the business as collateral and walk away with cash. If you've built a profitable business by the time you're ready to retire, you're in great shape!

Recommendation #3: Raise Independent Children

Adult children who are still living at home are a huge impediment to retirement! Even worse are adult children who bring a slew of children with them. Imbue in your children the expectation that they make their own way in life.

I knew that my father expected me to move out of the house at the age of eighteen. He told me early and often about the realities of aging and that the day would come when he could no longer work. He had to save enough money to care not only for himself but my mother as well. *"You don't want us moving in with you and your wife someday, do you?"* he'd ask.

He made it clear that as an adult, I was expected to have gainful employment and make my own way in the world and not be a drain on his finances.

It's amazing how quickly your adult children can make other arrangements when you set explicit expectations. If they know living with you (or off you) is not an option, they'll figure something out. They'll make it work.

While attending university, I found it very difficult to pay rent. As stated, I wasn't welcome to live at home. It was a difficult situation. But an opportunity presented itself. There are situations in which established people leave home for extended periods of time. They need someone to house sit for them. I found one of these situations and offered my services. While housesitting for the first couple, I was approached by other couples who were facing the same situation. So, by the time the first couple returned home, I already had another housesitting opportunity lined up.

At one point after I was married and living in my own home, I was shocked to hear that a couple of my siblings had moved in with my parents. One was between jobs and the other was trying to save money before getting married. I wondered if my father had softened until my mother told me that one day he marched downstairs and gave both siblings an ultimatum. They were to be out of the house by a certain date or begin paying rent. Apparently, the quote for rent was rather exorbitant. They both moved out by the stated deadline.

Obviously, the younger your children are when you teach them to make money, save money, be resourceful and financially independent the better. If you haven't done it yet, there's no time like the present to explain to them what my father explained to me... and enforce it.

Recommendation #4: Invest In Income-Producing Assets

If you've paid off a home, built a profitable business and successfully weaned your children off your financial teat, you're in the top percentage of people in the world. You'll very likely to be able to retire comfortably when the time comes.

To really set yourself apart, take the next step of acquiring income producing assets. Obviously, real estate assets like rental units and commercial buildings come to mind. However, there are other income-producing assets that are far less risky and offer a much higher rate of return.

I'm not going to list or recommend these assets, but I'll offer an example of an income-producing asset that falls under this less risk, high return category to get your mind working.

At the age of 26, I got a call from my older brother. "Jeff, you've got to get yourself some vending machines!" He said excitedly. He went on to explain the financial math of his recent venture into the world of vending. His newly built route was doing exceptionally well. The vending machines in question were small gumball style machines placed in waiting areas inside restaurants. Instead of gumballs, his machines were filled with delicious Swedish mints.

The mints were round, about the size of a small gumball with a mint center, a chocolate coating and a harder candy coating over that. The cost of the four or five mints dispensed by the machine came out to about a nickel. To get the mints, customers inserted a quarter. That's a four hundred percent profit margin! Each machine, including a full globe of mints, cost roughly $125.

I decided to buy three machines and see if I could get them placed. One evening after work, I took a machine to my favorite restaurant in San Diego, California where I lived at the time. I experienced some trepidation as I waited for the maitre'd to retrieve the manager so I could ask permission to place my machine in the lobby. The manager looked my machine up and down for what seemed like a long time. Finally, she said, "We can give it a try. Stick it in lobby over by that tree." I thanked her and hurriedly moved in the direction of the tree. As I did, I felt her eyes boring into me from her perch at the top of the stairs. I was worried she was going to change her mind.

"Hey!" she said. My heart sunk as I waited for what came next. "Do you have another one of those things? I think one would do well downstairs in the bar."

"Sure," I said. "I can get another one."

"Get two more." she said. "We own the restaurant across the street, too."

Just like that, all three of my machines were placed. Each of my machines, all placed in high-end restaurants, averaged two hundred dollars a month net profit.

Within a month, I grew my route to twelve machines. Those twelve machines generated $2,400 in net monthly revenue. Our rent at the time was only $640 (which I thought outrageous), so the extra income from that route was a huge upgrade to our financial situation. Servicing my route was easily completed every Saturday morning before noon. It really was a great experience.

Personally, I'm not a fan of real estate rentals or rentals of any kind. Every time I loan something out, it comes back broken. I know that when you're in the rental business, you charge the customer for repairs and can even come out ahead on them. But now you're in the repair business and I don't want to be. The experience I had with vending machines opened my eyes to the sheer bliss of owning high-yield income producing assets, and taught me that there are simpler, less risky ways of doing it.

Recommendation #5: Don't Really Retire

My father loved owning commercial real estate rentals! For him, owning buildings was his hobby... a very profitable one. He understood the concept of buying fixer uppers too. He'd make low-ball offers on distressed properties and when one of his offers was accepted, he'd remodel and beautify the property to maximize its utility and curb appeal. Then he'd rent it.

Long after he sold his lighting supply company and "retired," he bought, fixed up and rented commercial real estate. Eventually, he hired a management company. So, the only managing he had to do was managing the manager, which he also loved doing.

My father puttered around his buildings into his early eighties. A few years before he passed, he turned the responsibility of managing the property manager over to my older brother. Even then, he'd read my brother's reports with great enthusiasm.

When my father passed, my mother was able to live out her days in comfort and dignity. She never had to move in with one of her children. I know my father took great pride in how well he'd set her up financially.

The point is this: Make as much money as you can and find something you can invest in that you love! If you can manage that investment into advanced age and you really enjoy doing it, then you never really retire.

I can't over emphasize the luxury of always having more income than expenses. If you meet with a financial planner, he or she will calculate what you're likely to have upon retirement and then formulate what's called a withdrawal strategy. Meaning, you've got what you've got, and now you start drawing it down, hoping you don't run out before you pass.

My father never worried about a withdrawal strategy because he never really retired. His is the best example of preparing for retirement that I have to draw on.

Recommendation #6: Move

If you've done the above, the chances are that you'll be able to retire comfortably in your home country.

But what if you haven't? What if you haven't saved millions of dollars? What if you haven't built a profitable business? What if you don't own a home? What if you have no income producing assets? What if you simply can't afford to retire in your home country?

Move!

I have friends who live comfortably on their $750 Social Security check in the English speaking, Caribbean country of

Belize. They've never been happier. They're healthier than they'd be living back home. They don't own a car, so they walk to the open-air market every morning where they buy their fresh produce. They have coffee on the balcony of their $300 dollar a month rental and keep in touch with family via Skype.

Now, it may not be the ideal situation. There are some things they miss out on. But they're retired. And they're not a burden on their children.

They buy $3 shirts and shorts at the same thrift stores the locals shop at. When needed, they get health care at the same clinic the locals attend. In other words, they get by exactly the way everyone else does in Belize.

Life for them is an adventure and they love it! They also have friends who own cars and are happy to provide a ride. Some of their friends are very wealthy. I, along with everyone else, know their situation. So, when I invite them out, it's my treat. They're living a very comfortable, peaceful and pleasant life.

The facts are, I've done most of the recommendations listed above and I'm still planning to retire on my farm in Belize.

Five days into each visit, I notice a remarkable improvement in my health. My sinuses clear up. I can breathe clearly and deeply. My energy elevates. By the time I return to the States, I've always lost a little weight. Why? Because even though I own a vehicle, I walk along the bay to the market every morning. In the town where I have a place, there are no fast-food chains. None. I eat only fresh fruit and vegetables and lots of farm-fresh scrambled eggs. That's all there is to eat! Thirty eggs cost $5 (US) in Belize! When I eat out, I order something with meat, but everything served is fresh. I drink coconut water from coconuts grown on my own trees. I eat produce that I rarely if ever eat in the States. Take pineapple for instance. The flesh of pineapples in the States is light-yellow, very acidic and not very sweet. In Belize, pineapple flesh has a deep golden hue and is sweet like a candy bar!

Now, you may think that you don't have enough money to even retire in a Third World country. Okay. Consider remote employment.

At first mention, remote employment seems to contradict the concept of retirement but hear me out. If you're living very inexpensively in a Third World country, you can generate the little you need in just a couple hours of remote work per day. If you do a search on YouTube for remote work, you'll find lots of good videos on how to obtain it.

Living in a Third World country may not be your first choice, but if it turns out to be your only choice, you may just find that you're happier than you've ever been.

Conclusion

Retirement seems very far away when you're young. So, many people don't properly plan for it. By the time people feel their bodies and minds slow down and the reality of retirement descends upon them, it can feel like it's too late.

Obviously, the earlier one faces the reality of retirement and begins earnestly preparing for it the better. Retirement should be a time of peace and enjoyment. I hope the above recommendations help you achieve that situation. Either way, remember. Just as young adults can become very resourceful and figure things out if the expectation is set for them to do it, you can also figure out how to retire once you set your mind to it. The trick is to set your mind to it now!

Best of luck!

About Jeff Buehner

A highly successful entrepreneur and #1 bestselling author, Jeff Buehner attributes his success to the writings of Sultan Musa of Mali, one of the richest men to live.

32 years ago, Jeff worked himself to exhaustion as a concrete contractor with little to show for it. A kindly, elderly woman introduced him to the Sultan's writings. Contained in these writings is something called the language of the gods. Musa said, "Anything uttered in this language, the world obeys your commands."

Having nothing to lose, Jeff began speaking this language. Almost immediately, strange "coincidences" began popping up and they continued popping up until everything Jeff said in this language became his reality. One of the most poignant lines in Jeff's book, *The Sultan's Seven Secrets*, is when Jeff says, "At one point, money, opportunity, homes, cars and other material things came so fast that I actually used the language of the Gods to slow things down a bit." That's how powerful this is! In his book, Jeff holds nothing back explaining exactly how to speak the language of the Gods and what to expect when you do.

https://sultansjourney.com/

The Sultan's Seven Secrets (Amazon) *https://amzn.eu/d/8QAclp*

The Real Retirement Challenge

Andrew Priestley

Let me start by confessing something: in early 2023, I was in no shape to walk any distance – let alone under a blistering 35-degree Spanish sun, up the endless rugged hills of northern Spain.

But when a good friend invited me to walk the last section of the Frances Camino de Santiago, I said yes because ever since a friend of mine walked the entire Camino – and loved it – and after I'd seen the Camino movie,'The Way', I realised something deeper had been nudging me for some time. Maybe I felt the need for a challenge. An adventure. Or maybe it was just curiosity – or the romantic pull of a pilgrimage.

In any case, I realised I was nowhere near fit – or even conditioned enough – for an eight-hour-a-day, ten-day walk. I needed to lose two stone and rediscover the part of myself that once moved with more ease. There was no way I was going to haul 13 stone around Spain!

With that as a goal, I started training seven months out. Every day, I walked 3-5 miles. And that first decision quietly influenced the entire rhythm of my life.

The Wake-Up Call

Like many busy professionals in their 50s and 60s, my days were full and long – coaching clients, leading workshops, speaking at events, fielding constant emails. Desk bound. I wasn't exactly unhealthy, but I wasn't thriving either. The creeping weight gain, the mental fatigue, the sluggishness… long nights watching TV… it had all become normal. And that's the danger, isn't it? When average replaces optimal and we just call it "getting older."

My older sister had needed to change her diet and lifestyle. An arthritis sufferer, the motivation was to be pain-free. She cut out all foods renowned for causing inflammation. Within weeks, she started to feel miraculously pain-free and went from being on nine types of medication… to one within three months. But an unexpected benefit was weight loss. She dropped two stone.

A good friend – a highly qualified Chinese Medicine practitioner - took one look at me and said, "We need to clean up your liver and gall bladder." Not exactly the pep talk I expected, but I listened.

She put me on a morning smoothie regime of cucumber, celery, apple and carrot. Within a couple of weeks I could feel my whole system reenergising. Within two months, I had lost one and a half stone and felt sharper, lighter, stronger.

By the time I hit the Camino trail, I was in the best shape I'd been since my early 40s. The hills were very steep, the tracks were unmade and rough, and the southern European sun was relentless – but I cruised through it.

I looked good, felt amazing, had dropped two suit sizes and did not want to go back to that old way of being.

I started thinking about lifestyle choices that involve adventure.. and semi retirement. And I noticed the subtle shift to thinking about long term health and wellbeing. That was the real revelation.

Rethinking Retirement As A Performance Challenge

To be clear, I'm not in the health or wellbeing sector. I'm not a health guru. I'm not selling supplements or a wellness plan. I'm an executive coach qualified in Industrial and Organisational Psychology with a lifelong fascination with peak performance.

Most of my clients are established professionals: founders, executives, leaders in their field. But too many of them, right now, frankly, aren't in good shape. Most are punished by demanding work commitments: unhealthy, sleep-deprived, undernourished, and chronically overstimulated. And they drink too much, scroll too often, yet work like they're invincible.

This experience – training, getting fit, walking the Camino, feeling re-energised – started to make me more intentional about long term lifestyle, health and energy choices.

If I raise the topic of healthier choices in conversations with my clients generally they say things like: "I'll deal with all that... when I retire."

Except they won't because it isn't a focus or a priority, now. And right now, they're too exhausted or disconnected to consider the longer term scenario. My top five clients are all 5–10 years from the traditional retirement age of 65. And in all cases, the common worry is health issues.

I studied sports psychology and the wellbeing domains that underpin peak performance for athletes are:

- General health
- Physical activity
- Nutrition
- Rest
- Biomechanics
- Mental energy

I realised my clients have the money but aren't fit to retire. The irony is people who are smart enough to think strategically about their businesses, don't – or won't – prioritise their personal lives. In sports coaching we ask: what is your performance vision; and what's getting in the way?

My clients talk about:

- Food related issues (poor diet, mindless eating)
- Poor rest and recovery (broken sleep, sleeping less and less)
- Diminished or absent sex life
- TV binge-watching anxiety and fear-based content (to 'rest'!)
- Device madness (email, social media, mindless scrolling, browsing including porn)
- Emotional distractions (gossip, sensational news)
- Relationship issues (reduced human connection)
- Hormone issues (more on that another time)

While intellectually, all of them say they need to think about health and wellbeing… it just isn't today.

My own encouraging experience of losing weight and getting back into shape in my sixties, had me exploring: what if I approached retirement planning the way elite athletes approach competition? Not as a wind-down, but as a peak event.

Something I should train for.

Most professionals know they need to "plan" for retirement. The financial side gets prime attention – pensions, investments, maybe a property or two – but the health and wellbeing side it typically ignored. There's no game plan.

Nothing intentional.

That was me. I want financial stability - for sure - but I now want adventure and the health and vitality to really enjoy it.

My Version Of A Fit Retirement

This is my current focus and best thinking. A framework I've identified – for me personally – that I've been exploring as I contemplate semi-retirement.

1. Physical Health & Movement

Not just "exercise," but functional movement, joint health, flexibility, and strength. Can you walk five miles without pain? Squat to tie your shoes? Climb stairs without wheezing? These things matter – because retirement isn't about sitting still. For me it's about deliberately and intentionally staying mobile, active, engaged.

2. Nutrition And Metabolic Health

Your body is a chemistry lab. What I eat (and drink) affects everything – my energy, mood, cognition, immunity. A liver/gall bladder cleanse may not be for you, but resetting my food habits felt like I turned the clock back 20 years.

3. Recovery And Rest

Sleep. Downtime. Screen breaks. Think of them not as luxuries, but as strategy. Rest isn't passive – it's productive. In fact, most growth (physical and mental) happens during recovery, not during the grind. And I need rest.

4. Mental Focus And Emotional Energy

Our attention is under siege. Emails, news alerts, social media all demanding a slice of your brain. Professionals need a plan to reclaim focus. For me that meant mindfulness, journaling, prioritising hobbies, or simply turning off, and going off-grid for periods of the day.

5. Purpose And Identity Beyond Work

This is the big one for me. Meaning and purpose. For me, it got me thinking about contribution and legacy.

I have had several part-time passion projects. I've mentored people. And I've prioritised learning something new like cooking. I cannot underrate the importance of clarifying meaning and purpose at this vital stage of life. So, what gives you meaning when there are no meetings in the diary? Many professionals delay these questions until it's far too late.

6. Fun

This means enjoyment, joy and an excitement about life. It means I have become more intentional and conscious about what I want to do that is fun.

These were six themes highly relevant to my life, right now. Yours might be different.

From Strategy To Action

What I've found is that most people don't need convincing - they need structure. They need a shift in mindset that reframes a healthy retirement not as "the end" but as a lifestyle. And something worth investing in.

Start simple. Start with the obvious. Audit your health. (Have a full health check-up. Review your weekly habits. Choose your own five domains and give them focused attention. Get expert help if you need it – a coach, a nutritionist, a physio, a doctor, a specialist. For me I invested in top shelf blood tests.

In any case, great health was stamped Urgent.

Final Thoughts From the Trail

I didn't expect the Camino to change my perspective on retirement. But it did.

There's something about walking – step after step, hour after hour – that strips away your distractions. You start hearing your own thoughts again. Bit by bit I realised how vital it is to stay fit, focused, and fuelled. I enjoyed my leaner body. I was secretly smug that I cruised up very steep mountain paths. It made me deeply reflect on my lifestyle and health and wellbeing choices. I want to enjoy my retirement. When it comes.

Whether you're 45, 55 or already in your early 60s, let me offer this encouragement: You don't need to have it all figured out. But put it on the agenda. And pay attention to what seems obvious and important to you right now.

My long term change started with the goal of a short walk in Spain. It might be something as. simple as that for you, too.

About Andrew Priestley

Andrew Priestley is qualified in Industrial and Organisational Psychology, an award-winning seasoned business leadership coach, a respected non executive director for established multi-generational family businesses, a best selling author and an in-demand speaker.

He is committed to coaching leaders to lead 'well above the line'. If you are not sure what that means, then perhaps connect with Andrew.

www.andrewpriestley.com

https://www.linkedin.com/in/andrewpriestley

Retire Inspire 1 is also available on Amazon

Ebook

https://amzn.eu/d/bQwQrWE

Paperback

https://amzn.eu/d/ejB4BJa

If you would like to contribute to *Retire Inspire 3* please email *coachbiz@hotmail.com*

Printed in Dunstable, United Kingdom

66190846R00122